BRIDGER

What
World-Class
Innovators Do

Bridger: what world-class innovators do/B. Tom Hunsaker.
ISBN 978-0-9985186-3-3
1. Leadership. 2. Innovation 3. Organizational Change. 4. Management.
Cataloging-in-Publication Data for his book can be obtained from
Library of Congress

1 2 3 4 5 6 7 8 9 0

BRIDGER

What
World-Class
Innovators Do

PREMIER DEVELOPMENT EDITION

B. Tom Hunsaker, PhD

CONTENTS

PREMIER DEVELOPMENT EDITION

This is the second of four volumes in the Premier Development series — bringing to life leading-edge methods and proprietary tools, applied the world over, focused on the key growth architecture dimensions: mindset, innovation, strategy, and execution

MAXIMIZE YOUR INNOVATION CAPACITY

How great innovators stand out from the crowd is no longer left to chance. Building on over a decade of primary research, applied experience and interviews with world-class founders and product innovators, comparative analysis spanning defining innovations across history, and pivotal secondary work from the neuro and social sciences, the evergreen Bridger approach (featured in **Harvard Business Review**) outlines the game-changer innovator difference.

The first Bridger innovation study was featured in

HARVARD BUSINESS REVIEW

PREFACE

Questions have power to ignite curiosity and imagination in ways statements alone don't.

Equally important is to recognize that successful behaviors are largely learned. How we engage, interact, and influence tend to be built — not simply born. This is the case with effectively innovating. The process is inclusive (nearly anyone can do it) and straightforward (it does not require an abundance of a particular resource). Perhaps most important, doing so doesn't necessarily depend upon changing one's surroundings or the participants in it.

Following this pattern, this work began with the question:

— What do world-class innovators do differently and how can these skills be successfully transferred to others?

Grounded in over a decade of primary research, secondary studies of the breakthrough innovations and their authors spanning, C-suite and founder lived experiences, and pivotal work from neuro and the social sciences, the case for what world-class innovators do is compelling. So much so that their common threads gave rise to a shared designation — Bridger.

Descriptions of phenomena are valuable, but they can frustrate when they're not actionable. *Bridger: What World-Class Innovators Do* is designed to not only be enjoyed, but applied. The hope is that this book feels approachable and aspirational — like it's written for you and provides a spark for what to do next (regardless of your starting point).

Filtering influential research through years of professional experience, this volume provides practical methods to greatly improve your innovation output. Consider this your personalized development platform as you come to embody the Bridger skillset — and help others to do the same.

Ultimately, the value of something is found in its doing. All the genuine best as you embrace this invitation.

ACKNOWLEDGEMENTS

Henry David Thoreau once said, "Not that the story need be long, but it will take a long while to make it short." This book is years of input, iterations, and refinement in the making. During that time, over 1000s of case examples were analyzed, 10s of thousands of flight miles traversed, hundreds of interviews conducted, iterations published in leading outlets, dozens of experiments conducted. None of this would have been possible without an incredible network of colleagues and supporters. While it is impossible to list them all, there are several groups and individuals we do wish to acknowledge separately.

Lasting concepts are rooted in applied experience. Exhaustive study of innovators through the centuries — men and women who dared to stretch the boundaries of what was then the status quo — took me into many workshops, offices, labs, fields and galleries across the globe (some literally, others figuratively). More importantly, I was permitted into their thought and action patterns to uncover commonalities. Thank you for standing apart and for caring enough to document your journeys.

Winston Churchill was fond of saying, "I am always ready to learn, although I do not always like being taught." To the thousand plus graduate students in my classes through the years, thank you for being ready to learn and willing to be taught. You have been curious, thoughtful, and insightful. Most importantly, you've shown the value of being 'interested' over merely 'interesting.'

To the many who provided me a living laboratory to observe behaviors and validate ideas, thank you for trusting this work's process before it was fully formed and for dedicating countless hours to its refinement. You readily applied concepts in your work, your families, and your relationships and then had the audacity to share what you experienced. This effort would not have been possible without your contribution.

This work was presented in hundreds of formats before taking the shape of a book. I sincerely appreciate all those who approached me with their comments and insights. Your successes and encouragement provided a deep reservoir to draw from when words didn't want to emerge.

It is not uncommon for manuscripts of this nature to linger in a complex state without skilled editorial support. I'm grateful to those who spent many hours helping to shape this work into its present form.

This journey has dotted the globe. Along the way, I've observed humanity at its finest.

It is said that no one accomplishes anything worthwhile without the support of a true confidant. Thank you to my dear wife for the many late-night conversations, for poking at prodding my writing to the point of refinement, for wearing many hats while I was away, and for the steady belief in this message and its messenger. You inspire me beyond words.

To those who dare to
see what others miss,
and bring these ideas
to life

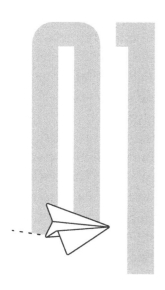

DYNAMISM

It can be tempting to view successful enterprises as nameless systems. Or, to assign their performance to entitlement or chance. But all have histories of key moments traced to people who saw something that others missed and got their ideas implemented when others couldn't. The last century has produced especially compelling cases of individuals influencing their firms' course, among them a key growth insight for Walmart.

Walmart is among the world's largest firms by number of employees and annual revenues.[1] Environmental destiny does little to explain this success. The company didn't exist before 1962, it is headquartered outside the United States' primary industrial clusters, and it operates in the less glamorous volume-based retail sector. How did Walmart make the leap from small local store in Rogers, Arkansas to one of the world's largest companies?

From a distance, many viewed the firm's founder, Sam Walton, as a folksy ideologue — a simple man better suited to outwork a challenge than to innovate through it. A closer look reveals that he was the opposite; consistently observant of opportunities to

---

1   "Walmart". *Fortune*. Global 500. Retrieved August 12, 2019.

catalyze the business — regardless of their source. This approach was pivotal to Walmart's trajectory twenty years after its founding when Walton spotted an idea on a trip to Europe that would revolutionize the firm's distribution system and allow it to scale in ways previously unimagined in the retail industry.

While walking through a Marks and Spence store in Great Britain, Walton noticed the flowers they sold were uncommonly fresh. Curious, he asked the store clerk how this was done. The clerk introduced Sam to the store manager who showed him a simple software program that allowed the store to connect smoothly with suppliers–greatly reducing inventory cycles and costs.

When he returned home, Walton prioritized tailoring the essence of what he'd observed in Europe. He met with several of his managers and key leaders from P&G (then one of Walmart's largest suppliers) to build interest in the concept. Walton picked one product (pampers) and tasked his technology team to work with P&G executives to create a program that allowed Walmart to send real-time data to P&G for inventory replenishment–setting in motion what would become the world's foremost retail distribution system. This breakthrough enabled the firm to scale and enter product categories that were previously unimaginable. Walton didn't just see fresh flowers. He saw the opportunity they represented.

Thousands of other retail executives walked similar streets in Europe before Sam Walton. But he saw what they missed. And doing so gave rise to an unparalleled competitive advantage.

Walton is an example of the power of Bridgers — skilled conduits for valuable ideas.[2] Transcending the underwhelming organizational mold of isolated, one-way innovation efforts Bridgers effectively observe their surroundings for promising opportunities, test them to identify their distinct advantages, and

---

2   The concept of *Bridgers* was first introduced in Harvard Business Review. Washburn, N. T., & Hunsaker, B. T. (2011). Finding great ideas in emerging markets. *Harvard Business Review, 89*(9), 115-120.

skillfully win their adoption. As operating environments grow more dynamic the need to infuse managers with Bridger skills increases.

DYNAMISM — NOW AND THEN

Consider the modern era's speed of change. In just fifteen years Apple rose from near bankruptcy to the most loved brand in the world. During that same period IBM went from top three most loved brand to nearly dropping out of the top fifteen. GE fell out of the rankings altogether after spending several years in the top five. Google went from unranked in the top fifteen to second globally.[3]

Dynamism is even more dramatic when viewed through the lens of particular inventions. Products can catapult from non-existence to creation to near ubiquitous adoption with remarkable velocity. Take the decade between 2010–2019, for example. In just ten years the following products went from unconceived to deep adoption: iPad, Instagram, Square, Slack, Pinterest, GPS, Air Pods, Microsoft Surface. Add one more decade cycle and industry had yet to develop any smartphones, functional Wi-Fi, any social media platforms, podcasts, Bluetooth, e-readers, Netflix or other on-demand digital entertainment applications, YouTube or derivatives, or nearly all of the fintech, AI, or machine learning capabilities heavily present in industry and beyond.

The velocity of information development and dissemination may be more remarkable. By 2019 the 2.5 quintillion bytes of data threshold had been surpassed — daily. Broken down by *every minute*, that included nearly 4 million Google searches, close to 4.5 million YouTube video views, approaching 500,000 tweets, and nearly 100,000 hours of Netflix user streams. These numbers only scratch the service of the amount of data to be generated going forward. The Internet of Things (IoT) accelerates data production at such pace that over 90 percent of the data in the world

---

3   https://www.youtube.com/watch?time_continue=60&v=tOOachJXSJM&feature=emb_
    title (Retrieved December 11, 2019).

is produced less than every two years. For perspective, all the information in recorded human history prior to 2019 accounted for barely 10 percent of the data generated from 2018–19.

While the speed of change and angles from which change emerge has radically increased with digital connectivity, the principle of dynamism is not new.

In 1839, China was one of the largest, richest, most effectively governed states in the world. However, when the outnumbered British Royal Navy attacked costal cites and forts, the Chinese fell to superior British muskets and cannons which fired more rapidly and accurately than their own firearms. The result of the superior British weapons was that China lost its sovereignty and dominant status in the world's hierarchy for almost a century. The irony of this tragic experience is that guns and gunpowder were originally Chinese inventions. The British (and other European countries) took something very Chinese, adapted it and then used it to confront the inventor.

Gunpowder was discovered by Chinese alchemists and introduced to the Chinese military around 1200 A. D., but the entrenched military leaders failed to fully embrace and improve this technology. The relatively stable, centralized Chinese government lead by a series of inwardly-looking emperors did not require radical changes in their military tactics. In contrast, when guns and gunpowder spread to Europe (a collection of warring nations without a true political center) the new technology was rapidly embraced. In this fractured and then fringe environment, guns and gunpowder evolved into efficient military weapons. Lead bullets, muskets, and the corning of gun powder (wetting gunpowder to form small pellets that made it more stable) are examples of some of the advances made in this context. By the 1800s advanced firearm technology was being used across Europe.

And so, when England attacked China, it was with a Chinese invention that had been modified by the agitation and necessity of the European context. China, with all of its advances in administration and civilization did not stand a chance. China's failure to keep pace with the Chinese-spawned but European-modified technology led to China's defeat.

The story ended differently when England waged war against a small, disorganized, fringe country in 1776. This was in part because the soon to be United States had taken the Chinese-spawned European-modified invention and made it uniquely American. Hunting for game in wooded frontier land called for longer range accuracy so rifling was invented (spiral groves inside the barrel that cause bullets to spin), and with it the practice of 'sharp shooting' which enabled the 'under-sophisticated' Americans to take out British officers from longer ranges. This innovation was a significant contribution to the United States' upset of the English Empire.

In each historical case and throughout modern time the roots of vital innovation trace to someone (or a few people) able to harness information and see valuable opportunities others miss, quickly and effectively validate to strengthen decisions, and win idea adoption. The result is their teams, organizations, cities, agencies, and even countries and regions, uniquely thrive compared to their would-be peers.

But there is something more to this pattern — something fundamental to success that can be learned and repeated.

BRIDGER PLAYBOOK

How great innovators stand out from the crowd is no longer left to chance. Building on nearly a decade of primary research involving hundreds of enterprises and many more managers, applied experience and interviews with world-class founders and product innovators, comparative analysis spanning defining innovations across history, and pivotal secondary work from the neuro and social sciences, the Bridger approach outlines the gamechanger innovator difference.

Just as software depends on the quality of input information to succeed or fail in its job, innovation capacity is less a function of genetics and more a set of learned behaviors. Knowing how to do this well (and to teach others to do the same) fundamentally impacts most conceivable innovation quality measures.

The remaining chapters provide applied frameworks, practical understanding, and grounded methods (with emphasis on usability) — for decoding and effectively putting to action a world-class innovator's playbook.

Discovery section →

Part I: Respond

Respond to the questions below using the following rating scale:
A = Very likely.   B = LIkely.   C = Neutral.   D = Unlikely.   E = Very unlikely.

1. How likely are you to be excited when considering the world's dynamism?

2. How likely are you to see meaningful change as positive?

3. How likely are you to consider yourself capable of a gamechanger innovation?

Part II: Describe

For the following questions, describe how you would most likely respond. To get the most from your efforts, **don't** describe what you *think you should do*, but rather *what you would most likely actually do* based on how you've responded to similar situations in the past.

A close colleague asks you for your candid thoughts on the state of the world, its pace of change, and positive vs. frivolous change. How would you respond?

Suggested responses to Part I: A, A, A

How was your thinking influenced by this chapter? If you were asked to explain to others the positive aspects of dynamism, what would you share?

Practice Activities Section

Choose an industry and consider its dynamic development arc over the last 200, 20, and 2 years. This can be from your current work or another area of interest. For example, if you work in the medical industry you may consider the patient visit experience.

Step #1 — What are key elements in the Before, During, and After experience?

200 years ago, how did this industry look?

■ Political and Regulatory Landscape

_____

_____

_____

_____

■ Relevant Social Influences

_____

_____

_____

_____

■ Technological Landscape

_____

_____

_____

_____

■ Consumer Experience

_____

_____

_____

_____

20 years ago, what were some of the key innovation breakthroughs?

2 years from now what innovations are shaping the industry's development?

What are some drivers influencing the industry's current state?

FUTURE
SHAPERS

The heavy British accent is unmistakable as a reporter leans forward and asks a young girl to project into the future, "Who would you want to be like?"

The story is set in the backstreets of Compton, California. Known globally for its social challenges, Compton's poverty rate has historically been among the highest in America.[4] Property and violent crime rates reach are similarly poor. During the decade in which this young girl grew up, a resident of Compton was over ten times more likely to be murdered than those from neighboring cities in southern California.

The first thing to strike the reporter is the young girl's sport of choice. There is little about Compton's environment that would prompt a child to play tennis. Few public courts exist, and those that do are worn (mainly from neglect). It's not a common sport among school-aged children so there are few social reasons to take it up. Compton is a city often correlated with the toughest urban challenges from economic neglect and opportunity void to gangs and failing schools.

---

4   http://quickfacts.census.gov/qfd/states/06/0615044.html. Retrieved December 30, 2015.

Yet day after day this young girl worked at her craft along with her sister and father. Neither cracked courts nor crack houses would deter from the goal to use tennis to change her environment.

She would become one of the sport's all-time greats.

Serena Williams is a naturally gifted athlete. But so are thousands of other children in any city around the world. And, many of them grow up in better environments with access to more resources.

What makes her unique was foreshadowed many years before she first took the court for a professional tournament when that reporter asked her as a young girl who she wanted to be like.

"Well, I'd like other people to be like me."[5]

The young Serena's wry smile and direct eye contact as she said those words hinted that she really believed them. Her astounding success over decades as a tennis professional are the evidence.

At a very young age she understood something that eludes most. Environment is a powerful force, but not so powerful that individual agents can't shape their course within it — thereby, possibly, shaping the environment itself. This is even more the case when the operating terrain is dynamic — filled with movement, shifts, and disruptions that new entrants can seize for openings or savvy incumbents can harness to drive continuous innovation.

Shaping the future begins with the belief that the future can be shaped. And, you can do the shaping. This is where innovation success begins — and ends. This initial belief forms a key element of *enterprising capital* — the confidence component to effectively producing organized value.[6] Productively standing out in the face of forces pulling towards the familiar, ordinary, and average is foundational to innovation genesis and Bridger success.

---

5   https://www.youtube.com/watch?v=3K_4LfzKPko. Retrieved November 23, 2015.

6   Hunsaker, B. T. (2019) Autonomous University Strategy. Enterprising Capital c Hunsaker BT. Innovation Bridgers: The new talent imperative. Thunderbird Int. Bus. Rev. 2020; 1–8..

STANDING OUT, FOR GOOD

The common path is to use social benchmarking to determine what's possible (framing your potential by comparing yourself to your surroundings). More than seeking reference points to make sense of the world around you, this form of comparing passively outsources to the social environment your future prospects. Think of an airplane that is operating on autopilot. Rather than intentionally charting its course, it floats through the air in a subconscious-like state — waiting for someone to provide the next set of directions.[7]

In the common path your best prospect is to become the *average* of the environment in which you reside.

To anyone who has walked the hallways of a formal education institution in any number of countries or observed meeting interactions in randomly selected companies this is clear.

The other path is to consciously seek impactful innovation as you chart an intentional direction. Different from a personality trait, which is described as inherent or fixed,[8] this capability is surprisingly malleable — nearly anyone can do it and doesn't require a lot of time or specialized technical training.[9] Perhaps most important, doing so doesn't depend on changing your surroundings or the participants in it.

FUTURE SHAPER CASES

JEFF BEZOS: AMAZON

Amazon was founded in 1994 by Princeton graduate and former wall street vice-president, Jeff Bezos, who quit his job and moved to Seattle to participate in the internet boom of the time. By 1995 he had

7   Singelis, T. M. (1994). The measurement of independent and interdependent self-construals. *Personality and Social Psychology Bulletin, 20*(5), 580-591.

8   Bouchard, T. J. and McGue, M. (2003), Genetic and environmental influences on human psychological differences. J. Neurobiol., 54: 4−45. doi: 10.1002/neu.10160

9   Yeager, D. S. & Dweck, C. S. (2012). Mindsets That Promote Resilience: When Students Believe That Personal Characteristics Can Be Developed. Educational Psychologist, 47(4), 302−314, 2012.

launched Amazon.com to sell books online — fueled by the notion of the 'virtual' warehouse that allowed for wider selection without the cost of extensive inventories. Envisioning the internet's broader reach, shortly thereafter Bezos created a list of more than 20 products he thought could be successfully sold online. The company's IPO in 1997 under the symbol AMZN further capitalized the expansion of book sales and allowed the company to market other merchandise. Over the next decade Amazon prioritized volume and market share growth over profitability, a strategy supported by patient investors. By the early 2000s Amazon had developed the reputation for convenient online shopping featuring a vast array of products.

2013 marked the beginning of a meteoric valuation climb for the company, fueled largely by growing global interest in the digital economy and Amazon's ability to leverage its retail position to support ancillary digital offerings in media, cloud computing and more through Amazon Web Services, and a bevy of other sectors. In addition to price accessibility and sales growth the company focused extensively on customer convenience and loyalty. Amazon Prime provided unlimited two-day purchase deliveries and a range of ancillary services (e.g. online movie viewing) first in the United States and then in a variety of other countries for an annual fee. Experiments with aerial drones and other proprietary delivery services sought to reduce the company's input costs and enhance customer value.

Amazon Go reimagined the customer buying experience in altogether new ways by focusing on physical locations with self-serve virtual check out. Employing *Just Walk Out Shopping Technology*, Amazon Go introduced customers to the ability to completely bypass check lines. One industry analyst for RBC Wealth Management described, "Almost like the experience of shoplifting, except it's legal, and you don't need to hide the stuff in your jacket. ... Its in-store technology enables shoppers to have a very efficient and pleasant shopping experience. ... The overall opportunity is huge."[10]

10 https://www.forbes.com/sites/andriacheng/2019/01/13/why-amazon-go-may-soon-change-the-way- we-want-to-shop/#4dbc86a76709 Retrieved May 26, 2019

While still emerging, Amazon's investment rate and publicity efforts signal the firm is keen to expand this offering.[11]

JERRY CUOMO: IBM BLOCKCHAIN

By 2014, bitcoin was on its way to global recognition. Less familiar was the trusted transaction engine that powered it. Jerry Cuomo, then a CTO (chief technology officer) for IBM's middleware business, took interest in the underlying blockchain technology and (together with other IBM technologists) quickly envisioned significant potential for supply chain and other interactions.

— When I really got to see what was happening under Bitcoin, I got excited, as excited as anyone on the crypto side. But I was really excited about applying this to other uses. IBM certainly caters to business and enterprise. I became very curious about how we can apply this technology to allow businesses to collaborate. It seemed like this could be a unique way to transform a supply chain, on one side of the fence, or how trade financing works, on the other side of the fence. We got the spark of what could be. You're trying to set up a decentralized network between institutions, but this institution needs to be accountable. I need to be able to prove to an auditor that these events took place and I behaved this way. That's what started making us scratch our heads. How do we do this with the conventional blockchain? We came up with a set of ideas and we tried to apply them to Ethereum (an open-source, public, blockchain-based peer-to-peer computing platform and operating system featuring smart contract functionality). We ran into a couple of roadblocks, one being the lack of modularity in the early code base of Ethereum. The other is the licensing model. It was an LGPL license. In IBM, or in any institution that wants to commercialize something, it would be very hard to commercialize something with an LGPL license. Last but not least, there was really no unified governing board for Ethereum. We decided we needed to take another path. Together with Linux we formed the Hyperledger Project and built the blockchain business from the ground up.[12]

With Hyperledger, IBM learned from some of the improvements Ethereum had made while introducing innovation to underlying blockchain fundamentals.

---

11 https://www.forbes.com/sites/jonbird1/2019/04/14/bezos-on-amazon-just-a-small-player-in-global- retail/#2c556a8e4e76 Retrieved May 28,2019

12 Takahashi, Dean, "How IBM Will Use Blockchain as its Commerce Backbone" Venture Beat, 08 September 2018 https://venturebeat.com/2018/09/08/how-ibm-will-use-blockchain-as-its-commerce- backbone/

Convinced of blockchain's potential and encouraged by the engineering advancements achieved within the Hyperledger Project, IBM turned to creating use-cases for the technology. They looked specifically for higher-scale use-cases rife with inefficiency, waste, or questionable trust. Promising targets emerged within pharmaceutical trials, global shipping, and global food chains (among others).

Pharmaceutical companies spend tremendous sums to bring a new drug to market. A significant portion of the R&D investment goes toward clinical trials needed to provide evidence of intended-use drug efficacy and to receive approval to sell the drug. With the stakes for getting it right so high in medicine, regulators and honest broker firms have significant incentive to ensure unquestionable data record integrity. IBM saw a natural opportunity for blockchain's transparent and permanent transaction record to improve clinical trial trust.

Global shipping, specifically cargo, is essential but complex. Consider how much transaction record keeping is involved just to move one shipping container of a common item like salt. From place of origin to destination, and the ports in between, a record accounting for that product's movements must be kept. This cargo carries with it a trail of paperwork that can cost more to produce than the value of the goods inside — without being able to guarantee that nothing was altered or overlooked in the product's journey.

Perhaps most pressing given the industry's vital-nature and size was global food chains. Roughly one-third of the world's food supply chain is wasted. Food contamination alone cost the industry nearly $60 billion USD in 2016. Each incident of waste, spoilage, or tainting triggers a root cause analysis to uncover the problem's source. And each related inquiry must race against time to piece together records, perhaps from disparate sources, and rely on their integrity

These types of opportunities signaled to IBM that blockchain was more than interesting technology. Significant, pressing social and enterprise challenges could be solved by IBM's version of blockchain and related support.

THWAITES BROTHERS: CODA COFFEE USING MACHINE VISION, AND ARTIFICIAL INTELLIGENCE (AI)

Tim and Tommy Thwaites, founders of Coda Coffee, grew up in the coffee mecca of Seattle. In 1994, Tommy started working for Dillanos Coffee Roasters, at the time a startup themselves. In 1996, Tommy talked his brother, Tim, into joining the quickly growing Dillanos with a starting role of floor sweeper. After several years, Tommy became a vice president and Tim was promoted to roast master.

While working at Dillanos, Tim completed aviation studies with plans to become a commercial pilot. After the terrorist attacks on September 11, 2001, Tim changed course. The brothers moved to Colorado where they worked for a different coffee roasting company. They both quickly became disillusioned by dishonest practices taking place, and quit. They had rent to pay, so Tim started selling insurance door-to-door and Tommy took a job selling mortgages. Tim recalled a pivotal moment when he had to make his first insurance sale after shadowing an experienced salesperson for several months: It was the first time I got to sell my own product and actually make some money. The company let us offer potential clients a free death and dismemberment policy as goodwill gesture. When my first live prospect answered the door, I told her "Look, I don't want to do this. I'm really sorry. Here's a free policy. I gotta go." At that time, I was in Alamosa, Colorado. I got on the phone and called my brother and said, "Hey, let's open a coffee roaster." We had already chatted about it and it seemed like the right time.

At the time, Tom Thwaites, Sr., the brothers' father, was having heart problems and had to retire early. Taking a leap of faith, he offered his entire retirement account balance ($150,000 from his 401k) to his sons and became their silent partner. In 2005, the brothers founded Coda Coffee in Denver, Colorado, as a local wholesale coffee company.

Influenced by their love of outdoors and the environment, and the importance of social responsibility, the brothers decided to create a business that would not only pursue the best coffee beans in the world, but that it would do so while protecting the environment and supporting sustainable farming as well. This meant that in addition to simply buying raw coffee beans, known in the industry as cherries, they also committed to working with farmers directly to improve bean quality, and they would pay them handsomely for their efforts.

In December 2011, Coda Coffee introduced its Farm2Cup certification program. To become certified, farmers received education on, and committed to, detecting quality defects and making improvement on overall bean quality. They did this through approaches such as switching bean varieties, adjusting irrigation, or diversifying crops on their land, to name a few. Certified farmers received significant premiums for their coffee so long as the coffee met quality standards and the farmers showed their commitment to continuous quality improvement practices. In addition to the focus on quality improvement, Coda encouraged farmers to give back to their communities, particularly in health and education. The company also made independent contributions to various community-centered initiatives.

Tim and Tommy Thwaites focused on working directly with coffee farmers and cooperatives to influence sustainable growing practices. Cooperatives were partnerships between multiple small-holder farmers. Sharing of best practices and healthy competition among smallholder farmers within the cooperative resulted in continuous improvements in coffee quality. Additionally, the cooperatives were able to provide coffee processing equipment such as mills and bagging equipment that would not be affordable for individual farmers. Finally, the cooperatives also served as a single point of contact for coffee sales that would not be achievable for many smallholder coffee farmers with only a few acres of coffee. This provided buyers like the Thwaites brothers the opportunity to sample a range of different coffee beans at a single location.

Committing to working directly with coffee farmers and cooperatives required significant travel and hands-on work. Tim Thwaites described their approach in simple terms: "We'll go down and try each farmer's coffee. When somebody's doing an amazing job, we'll try to figure out why their product is better. When we share that information with other farmers, the overall quality goes up for their communal coffee."[13] To do this at scale the brothers turned to Machine Vision and AI. The results were immediate and sweeping.

> — On the farmer level, it does a couple things. For one, we know who gets paid what, so that's good. Two, they get paid instantly. The bext360 box that we put in coffee communities prints a receipt. Farmers take that receipt to the co-op or distributor and they get paid instantly. So, we know which farmer supplied the beans and how much and when they got paid. Without this blockchain system in place, farmers typically have to wait at least 30 days for payment. And that's after fronting money during a six- to eight-week harvest period during which farmers have to pay their workers. So, this really helps solve a critical cash flow challenge for the farmers. On top of that, the AI system provides great data on coffee quality.

COMMONALITIES

The Bridgers in these cases share common future shaping patterns. Each was open to the possibility that they could author something more valuable than what currently (or previously) existed. This prompted them to harness what others missed, connect dots in valuable ways with potential for unique advantages, and exhibit a scrappiness and resilience in the face of difficulty. They also share patterns for winning adoption for their ideas.

The *how* behind these patterns comprise the remaining chapters. Equally important to the insights, models, and frameworks presented is to appreciate their intent: they are guiding principles best maximized by thoughtful agents rather than mechanical prescriptions likely to deliver outcomes on autopilot. The instrument and musician are intimately connected. Effective Bridgers come to know this personally. And, they shape the future as a result.

---

13 Siebrase, Jamie. "Coda Coffee Co." CompanyWeek, 8 Jan. 2017; companyweek.com/company- profile/coda-coffee-co. *Discovery section →*

Part I: Respond

Respond to the questions below using the following rating scale:
A = Always.   B = Often.   C = Sometimes.   D = Rarely.   E = Never.

4. How frequently do you look for ways to stand out rather than fitting in to the status quo?

5. How frequently would others close to you say you encourage them to voice their thoughts — even if different than the norm?

6. Do you envision yourself to be a future shaper?

Part II: Describe

For the following questions, describe how you would most likely respond. To get the most from your efforts, **don't** describe what you *think you should do*, but rather *what you would most likely actually do* based on how you've responded to similar situations in the past.

You're presented with the question, "Who would you want to be like?" Describe why that person should be you.

_____

_____

_____

_____

_____

_____

_____

_____

_____

_____

_____

Suggested responses to Part I: B, B, B

Now, step outside yourself. Choose someone you see as a future shaper. Why did you choose this person? What attributes stand out to you? What can you learn from this person's approach to future shaping?

- Who would you select?

- Why?

- What attributes do you admire in this person?

- What can you learn from this person's approach to future shaping?

Future shaping brief assessment

Use the following scales to respond to the following questions:

1= Strongly disagree   *3= Neither agree or*   *4= Moderately agree*
2= Moderately disagree   *disagree*   *5= Strongly agree*

ATTITUDE

1. I have a natural curiosity to learn about people different from me

(1)   (2)   (3)   (4)   (5)

2. I enjoy the opportunity to do something I have never done

(1)   (2)   (3)   (4)   (5)

3. It is easy for me to put myself in others' shoes

(1)   (2)   (3)   (4)   (5)

4. I have a positive outlook about the future

(1)   (2)   (3)   (4)   (5)

5. I enjoy bringing people together to achieve new things

(1)   (2)   (3)   (4)   (5)

BEHAVIOR

6. I seek to understand new ideas before I reject or embrace them

(1)   (2)   (3)   (4)   (5)

7. I ask great questions

(1)   (2)   (3)   (4)   (5)

8. I consistently look for valuable ways to do it better

(1)   (2)   (3)   (4)   (5)

9. I act decisively on good new ideas

(1)   (2)   (3)   (4)   (5)

10. I persist through challenges to make good ideas happen

(1)   (2)   (3)   (4)   (5)

Practice Activities Section

Take the opportunity to further consider your responses to the Future Shaping Brief Assessment.

For which questions did you respond Agree (4) or Strongly Agree (5)?

_____

_____

_____

_____

Consider each of these questions more fully. Using examples, what attributes, competencies, and/or approaches do you exhibit to support your responses?

_____

_____

_____

_____

_____

_____

_____

How could you more fully build on these strengths?

_____

_____

_____

_____

_____

_____

For which questions did you respond Neither Agree or Disagree (3)?

_____

_____

_____

Consider each of these questions further. Why do you think you didn't take a position one way or the other?

_____

_____

_____

_____

_____

_____

How could you more fully build these attitudes or behaviors?

_____

_____

_____

_____

_____

_____

_____

_____

_____

_____

For which questions did you respond Disagree (2) or Strongly Disagree (1)?

_____

_____

_____

Consider each of these questions more fully. What do you think stands in the way of you Agreeing or Strongly Agreeing?

_____

_____

_____

_____

_____

_____

Consider each of these responses individually. How would success look for you in the attitude or behavior?

_____

_____

_____

_____

_____

_____

_____

_____

_____

_____

IDEATION — SEE WHAT OTHERS MISS

Before Starbucks was a household name Howard Schultz, then an employee of the small company, went on a business trip to Milan, Italy. When he returned a week later, he came back with an idea that would revolutionize the coffee industry and turn Starbucks into one of the biggest success stories of modern business.

One thing that Howard Schultz had going for him (that coffee executives managing the Folgers or Nescafe brands did not) was a lack of personal interest in the current structure of the coffee industry. As a newcomer, he did not suffer from the blindness that comes from having all your personal interests tied up in a particular way of selling coffee.

The brightness of personal interests is powerful and can cause you to filter out ideas that don't fit your current narrative. Like looking at the sun — it can blind you to everything in its direct view. This is why many coffee executives spent time in Milan previous to Howard Schultz, and not one of them came away with the ideas he did. In fact, when Schultz returned to Starbucks with his idea, it was this blindness that prevented executives at Starbucks from getting behind the idea. He had to leave Starbucks, and then buy it back to overcome the company's blindness.

One important feature of this blindness is that it only affects the center of our gaze where our personal interests are tied up. But if we turn our gaze away from the glare created by our personal interests, our vision is much clearer. Great ideas that are outside our personal interests are much easier to spot — our peripheral vision is just fine.

An awareness about the blinding effects of personal interests help to diffuse this glare. Sam Walton could have gone to Europe with a skewed mindset — and he would have overlooked the simple observation that triggered a radical shift (and growth catalyst) in Walmart's approach to distribution. Instead, he acknowledged there is something to learn in all settings — and his surroundings reciprocated.

Effective ideation involves certain skills (outlined in subsequent chapters), but these skills have little effect if not built on a solid mindset foundation. More than a nice way of thinking, there are specific efforts that set the stage for breakthrough ideation. Innovators who do this well follow three practices.[14]

MENTAL SUNGLASSES

First, by recognizing the blinding effect of personal interests, they start to mentally filter out this glare. Self-awareness is a powerful psychological tool. You can begin to develop your sunglasses by writing down your personal interests (social, political, and economic sunk costs and lifestyle or emotional interests in the status quo) — those things you'll likely want to defend. Be as specific as possible. Managers who are more willing to admit personal interests are less likely to be blinded by them.

As an example of this: it is incredible that Blockbuster executives could not see the Netflix threat and the value it offered existing Blockbuster customers (in fact when Netflix offered Blockbuster

---

14 Hunsaker, B. T. (2020) Innovation Bridgers: The new talent imperative. *Thunderbird International Business Review.*

a 49% stake in the company back in 2000, Blockbuster refused). But you lay the classic case out for a group of MBA students and the missed opportunities and mistakes are glaringly obvious. This isn't just a case of 'hind-sight is 20/20.' This is a case of 'peripheral vision is 20/20.' Because the students do not have a stake in the game, it is easy for them to see the problems.

Excellent peripheral vision can give us a false sense of competence ('I can see everyone else's challenges; I should be able to spot my own'). What every seeker of great ideas comes to recognize is that the most relevant ideas (particularly those that represent shifts in your current line of business) will be very difficult to spot and realistically evaluate. And the longer your tenure in an organization, position, or place, the truer this becomes.

In order to combat this blindness, we all need to invest in a strong pair of mental sun glasses that filters out the glare from personal interests and allows us to seriously consider the most relevant great ideas.

TRANSLATORS

In connection with this self-awareness, there is a need to bring in other individuals who will constructively challenge your thinking. The benefit of engaging others and asking them for candid input is that they can help you see what you are missing. When selecting an individual to help you see what you might miss, select someone who will provide merit-driven input, whose personal interests are disconnected from the idea or someone whose interests don't compete with your own, but who also has enough insight and background in the industry to provide a competent assessment.

Contrast this with studies highlighting that people are most likely to first share new ideas with those they think will agree with them.[15] This builds a second layer of bias into ideation even before

---

15   Data compiled by the author during teaching experiments between 2011-2019 involving nearly 1,000 graduate students.

the idea is initially prototyped or tested. Taking this approach will likely lead you to what you *want* to see, rather than what you *ought* to see.

Consider the successful example from a Senior Manager of a global oil and gas conglomerate to highlight the power of effective translators. Abner, a long-tenured export-business- development manager responsible for much of Latin America, was frustrated by the company's loss of market share and decided to get to the bottom of it. He started by recruiting a colleague, Carlos Medina, to help him investigate.[16] Medina was a local distributor in Mexico. Seeking out a trusted and skilled "translator"—someone who not only speaks the local language but is also ensconced in the market—would prove valuable in uncovering the root cause of the issue and opportunities for innovation.

In this case, Portillo served as the Bridger. He sensed the need and, emboldened by it, set out to discover an innovative solution. He amplified his efforts by enlisting the help of a local translator, Medina. Portillo is fluent in Spanish, the local language, but he recognized that language is only a small part of understanding the external environment. Portillo opted to partner with Medina because Medina was objective in his assessment of ideas, knowledgeable about the various players, and had access to important information about the realities of the market. Together they observed customers, conducted interviews, and reviewed the feedback gathered. Medina then helped Portillo make sense of what they observed.

The problem with the firm's lubricants wasn't the formulation, but the size of the package. They discovered that many buyers preferred lubricants in five-gallon containers rather than the 55-gallon drums that the company sold. The smaller containers were used as backup supplies for long hauls and were more condu- cive to managing inventory in these cash-centric markets. In some instances, buyers cleaned out and filled smaller containers from

---

16   Not his real name to preserve his privacy.

the 55-gallon drums to make the product more portable. In others, buyers opted to not purchase the larger drums at all. Portillo and Medina deduced that decreasing the container size would improve utility to drivers, enhance inventory controls, and better parallel the financial practices in local end-user businesses.

After implementing this idea, market share of lubricant sales sharply improved and exceeded pre-decline levels in Mexico and Central America. The five-gallon option was also made available in important Asian markets and beyond. The firm has used the Portillo case and other similar experiences to develop a more formal approach to enhancing the ideation capabilities of their people.

FUTURE PICTURES

The third practice to building an effective ideation foundation is to envision yourself experiencing success in the new idea. When a new idea presents itself, rather than checking it against your current interests, take an optimistic view of the future and your own position within that future — consider what could be and your role in it. By psychologically embedding personal interest into the new idea, you transform it into a highly visible and attractive idea. A bit of ambition and willingness to take risks helps this process along.

Many people who are successful at developing great ideas are relative newcomers and don't have to struggle with personal interest blindness. But working with thousands of people over the years has shown that even those with longer tenure in a certain position, organization, or location can overcome this blindness. Self-awareness, getting the perspective of trustworthy others, and envisioning a positive alternative future, each contribute to helping scout great ideas, even in their core operation.

For example, consider the interactions with employees from a global express delivery company. On a business trip to China, the potential for a significant disruptive innovation in the way this company currently operates was identified (use neighborhood hubs where individuals pick up their packages– rather than having drivers deliver them to the doorstep). Pictures were taken to document the opportunity and shared with managers at the company.

The initial reactions were uniformly disparaging and dismissive. More importantly, the negative responses were loudest from employees who perceived their current job functions were most likely to be impacted by the new model. Comments ranged from "that would never work here" to "I hope we're not crazy enough to do something like that." After these initial reactions, an industry consultant was brought in to let the managers hear the consultant's own assessment of the opportunity. Shortly after, I had a conversation with the employees about the blindness that personal motivations create and had the managers envision themselves in a very positive position within the new business model (less reliance on home deliveries, a much smaller fleet of trucks, managing a collection of small retail/delivery counters, for example).

While not everyone was able to get behind the idea, the transformation was rather dramatic. The conversation shifted from disparaging and dismissive to one focused on understanding the value that customers, who are typically not at home when packages are delivered, would derive from this new type of service.

If you can recognize and neutralize your personal motivations and are open to the possibility that something better can be created, then you are ready to go out and start observing. The observations that end up generating great ideas tend to focus on customers and their experiences (including potential customers, ex-customers, non-customers, competitor's customers, etc.), organizational feasibility, and industries and their drivers.

Most people are tempted to begin their pursuit for great ideas by looking at internal processes, interactions with suppliers, and the tactics of competitors. But more productive is the late Steve Jobs' observation that "you've got to start with the customer experience and work backwards."[17] Apple didn't revolutionize the music, personal

---

17   May 1997, World Wide Developers Conference (online video) 52:15/52:22

computing, and communications industries by asking 'what cool technology can we build?' — but rather by asking 'what valuable problem (friction) is the customer experiencing and how can we uniquely solve it?' Great observers appreciate that the best insights will come from intimately understanding the customer experience and the dynamics of related industries. They also consider how to resource their ideas early on to improve the odds for success.

Famed innovator, Thomas Edison, is credited with the words, "There's a way to do it better — find it."[18] There's an assertiveness to his statement that must have spurred Edison's efforts beyond any force of self-doubt, operating environment concern, or other constraint. There's also a surety of ability likely forged through developing particular skills key to the innovator's success. He believed in imagining what didn't yet exist and invested in the skills to bring these ideas to life.

Simple, yet powerful, this statement is a wonderful transition to the next ideation chapters, which outline key techniques great innovators use to stand apart and find the better way. Emphasis is given to in practice narratives, applied frameworks, practical understanding, and grounded methods (with emphasis on usability) to bring ideation to life in user-friendly, transferrable ways. The desire is for you to be equipped to develop gamechanger ideas- in any situation.

---

18   1961 June 5, New York Times, Edison Bust Enters Hall
      of Fame as Sarnoff Delivers a Eulogy, Quote Page 34,
      Column 7 and 8, New York.   *Discovery section →*

Part I: Respond

Respond to the questions below using the following rating scale:
A = Always.   B = Often.   C = Sometimes.   D = Rarely.   E = Never.

7. I intentionally consider my personal interests and biases so they don't blind me to new opportunities?

8. Among the first people I tend to share new ideas with are those I believe will agree with me?

9. When seeking a new idea my first action is to see what others are doing?

Part II: Describe

For the following questions, describe how you would most likely respond. To get the most from your efforts, **don't** describe what you *think you should do*, but rather *what you would most likely actually do* based on how you've responded to similar situations in the past.

You're tasked with facilitating a session with your colleagues about the ideation elements in this chapter. What will you share?

_____

_____

_____

_____

_____

_____

_____

_____

_____

_____

_____

_____

Suggested responses to Part I: A, D, D

What insights did you gather from the chapter you can begin to implement to improve your ideation approach? If you were asked to explain to others the concepts "Mental Sunglasses," "Translators" and "Future Pictures" what would you share?

■ Insights to Implement

_____

_____

_____

_____

_____

■ Mental Sunglasses

_____

_____

_____

_____

■ Translators

_____

_____

_____

_____

■ Future Pictures

_____

_____

_____

_____

_____

Practice Activities Section

Take the opportunity to personalize the "Mental Sunglasses," "Translators" and "Future Pictures" concepts.

Step #1 — Write down some personal interests you'd likely want to protect. When would you likely get defensive about these interests? What personal biases do you have around these interests? Why? (e.g. "It would be hard for me to admit Artificial Intelligence could do elements of my job better because this could jeopardize my security").

MENTAL SUNGLASSES ("I could find it hard to X, because Y")

_____

_____

_____

_____

Step #1 — What would you look for when seeking an effective translator? Why?

TRANSLATORS

_____

_____

_____

_____

_____

Step #1 — When presented with a new idea that may compete with your personal interests or biases what role can Future Pictures play in overcoming these forces?

FUTURE PICTURES

_____

_____

_____

_____

_____

Step #2 — Provide a concrete example of developing Mental Sunglasses in practice. Choose one of the personal biases you described in Step 1. How could Mental Sunglasses keep you from deflecting an idea that may challenge this personal bias?

MENTAL SUNGLASSES

_____

_____

_____

_____

_____

_____

Step #2 — Who in your current set of colleagues or associates could be an effective Translator. Why?

TRANSLATORS

_____

_____

_____

_____

_____

Step #2 — Consider a recent idea you deflected. What role did personal interests or bias play in your reception of the idea? Place yourself in the position of benefiting from the new idea. If the idea is objectively potentially valuable, how does your thinking change?

FUTURE PICTURES

_____

_____

_____

_____

_____

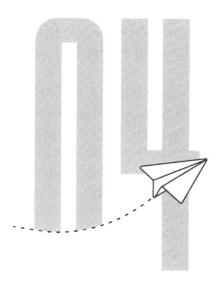

FIRST, WIN WITHIN

Lila Ibrahim, previous head of Intel's emerging markets platform group, shared during an interview, "Some managers believe in the potential for innovation, and others don't."

Few would openly admit that they're not interested in innovation, but intentions and actions don't always align. Mission statements are filled with language about innovation, Hallways carry creative images and slogans inviting passersby to innovate. And, goals often encompass innovation. Even the literature on change management outpaces continuity themes threefold. Yet, few actively and successfully seek out new enterprising ideas.[19][20]

Explaining this disparity begins with understanding the power of belief.

When Ibrahim assumed the leadership of Intel's emerging markets group, in 2007, its function was to provide technology for classrooms to support Intel's philanthropic investments in education. The group's efforts were one-directional and had

19   Washburn, N., & Hunsaker, B. T. (2011). Finding great ideas in emerging markets.

20   von Hippel, W., & Suddendorf, T. (2018). Did humans evolve to innovate with a social rather than technical orientation?. *New Ideas in Psychology, 51*, 34-39.

no revenue-driving innovation goal. Ibrahim came to believe that the unit could also create a low-cost notebook PC that would be a viable product for emerging markets.

She worked with a team, including social scientists, and had them spend time in Brazil, China, India, Nigeria, and elsewhere, analyzing local needs and preferences. Team members in Brazil heard from students that the PC should include a camera. Ibrahim didn't understand the logic of that request until she visited Brazil and saw that a camera would be an important way to make the computer what the students wanted it to be: a social tool that connected them with one another. She backed the idea—along with a suggestion that the camera be capable of moving—and she advocated for the experts' proposals regarding elements such as screen size, durability, and charging and wireless functions.

The resulting Classmate PC was the forerunner of the company's Netbook project, which created a new market for Intel in the segment of portable, durable, inexpensive, socially oriented PCs. (Intel doesn't build the computers itself; it produces the chips that power them and licenses other manufacturers to build them.) Intel has sold more than 90 million Netbook chips to ASUS and other companies.

Before skillset or technique, Ibrahim's success began by believing she could be a conduit for game changing innovations.

WHAT IF?

Because they vary from the norm, all new ideas are at first illegitimate. Engaging an action at first likely to be met with skepticism is a strong deterrent to would-be innovators. Adding to this challenge, otherwise would-be innovators can be heavily influenced by circumstance.

The example of the relationship between lottery activity, sporting event outcomes, and weather helps to illustrate this tendency. Researchers at New York University found significant correlation between experiencing a positive event (when a less positive outcome was expected) and participation rates in the lottery.[21]

The study looked at two years' worth of daily lottery purchases in 174 New York City neighborhoods. Citywide gambling increased following unexpected sports wins and unusually sunny days. In other words, when people expect a less desirable outcome than what actually occurs, they're more likely to double down on their *luck* and enter the lottery.

Though sporting event outcomes and weather have no rational bearing on likely lottery outcomes, experiencing a positive event that differs from what was expected — even if incidental — emboldens human behavior with belief in the potential for success.

While effectively innovating has nothing to do with weather or sports results, too often innovation efforts are treated whimsically — like playing the lottery when your team unexpectedly wins the game — believing in intermittent luck despite no rational grounding while silencing purposeful belief if no external prompt is present.

More powerful is to believe that each day there are great ideas to find — and you can find them; embracing the ethos, *learning is always the answer.*[22] And, then going about the real work to effectively do so.

BENEFITS OF BOLDNESS

During a conversation with a senior executive at German conglomerate Siemens, he expressed that one of his job's biggest challenges is to know when to stay the course and when to

21   Otto, A. R., Fleming, S. M., & Glimcher, P. W. (2016). Unexpected but incidental positive outcomes predict real-world gambling. *Psychological science*, 0956797615618366.

22   Hunsaker, BT (2018). Applied Learning – Social Proof of Mastery. Thunderbird Magazine.

change direction—before it's too late. He confided that this leaves him conflicted, and meaningful innovation often suffers.

He's not alone. IBM's Global C-suite Study of 12,854 participants from 112 countries outlines that nearly 70% of C-suite executives are largely concerned with a similar question.

Modern history is colored with examples of firms persisting when they should have changed course. Nokia, Guess, Relativity Media, and Gap are just a few examples. Resolve within a flawed pursuit won't deliver the intended outcome.

The same period saw puzzling examples of unrequited change — organizations shifting from a potentially promising course. This was the case when PepsiCo initially rebranded Tropicana, when Coca-Cola launched its New Coke initiative, and when Microsoft dramatically changed course from the popular XP system for the disastrous Vista (quickly needing to shift to the more stable and successful Windows 7), among others.

Just as some want the benefits of innovation, but struggle to believe they can be its author, others fear their efforts won't pay off and opt to maintain the status quo. Still others exhibit bias for whatever is new — without regard for whether it's better. All share a common core — they hinder valuable innovation before it's even developed.

More helpful is to develop an openness to the possibility that powerful innovation is within reach. The word *possibility* is important. Just as the fixed mindset will crowd out even the best ideas, the overly exuberant will embrace too fully the flawed. Win from within is an approach that reinforces the benefits, and discipline, of the bold mindset.

When YouTube violinist sensation Lindsey Sterling was asked, "You're very comfortable owning the spotlight. Any tips that [others] should know?" she gave an incredibly salient response supported by years of neurological research.

"Visualization—it's been huge for me. Your mind doesn't know the difference between imagination and reality. You can't always practice perfectly—my fingers will play a little bit out of tune or my dance moves might not be as sharp—but in my mind I can practice perfectly. Then it will be familiar to your brain."[23]

More than nice thoughts, the focused eye sees how thinking and doing intimately relate. The brain is beautifully intricate, but surprisingly simple. It is wired to process thinking about and actually experiencing an event in similar ways.[24][25][26][27]

This is why recalling an uncomfortable experience or personalizing a fictional film can ignite intense responses — as if you're living the event — despite knowing the experience isn't actually happening.

Because thinking and doing travel a similar mental pathway, patterns of thought have tremendous influence on actions. In the split second between impression and brain response, our thoughts impact how our brain functions. Consciously inserting certain thoughts, symbols, and visuals into your mindset prompts the brain to redirect resources to positive reinforcing functions.[28]

Consider an exercise successfully conducted with managers on four continents from companies like HP, Pfizer, Telekom, Movistar, SAP and GM to demonstrate how thought positioning can influence valuable new idea generation. Participants are shown the picture of a woman in the process of loading her car after finishing a shopping

23 http://www.glamour.com/inspired/2015/12/lindsey-stirling-highest-earning-female-youtuber. Retrieved December 9, 2015.

24 Jenkins, A. C., Dodell-Feder, D., Saxe, R., & Knobe, J. (2014). The Neural Bases of Directed and Spontaneous Mental State Attributions to Group Agents. *PloS one, 9*(8), e105341.

25 Saxe, R., & Young, L. (2013). Theory of Mind: How brains think about thoughts. *The handbook of cognitive neuroscience*, 204-213.

26 Bernhardt, B. C., & Singer, T. (2012). The neural basis of empathy. *Neuroscience, 35*(1), 1.

27 Saarela, M. V., Hlushchuk, Y., Williams, A. C. D. C., Schürmann, M., Kalso, E., & Hari, R. (2007). The compassionate brain: humans detect intensity of pain from another's face. *Cerebral cortex, 17*(1), 230-237.

28 Mindset is defined here as groups of thoughts that influence situational response and interpretation. There are many forces that influence one's mindset, including environment. In our observations, however, that relationship is not entirely deterministic.

experience and asked to describe an innovation to improve her experience. No further instructions are given.

Regardless of demographic or country, responses are predictable. Some struggle to come up with anything and conclude that they're not creative. Their thoughts tend to be negative reinforcers — worried about what they can't do or don't see. Their focus is to avoid making a mistake. And, this focus nearly guarantees they'll make the mistake of missing out on the potential for valuable new ideas.

Most of the other participants design innovations that are incremental, common, and oblivious to the cues from the woman in the picture. They struggle to adapt, automatically reaching for familiar ideas they've formed over years of experience that color how they process even new events.

Without providing innovation hints or ideas, a series of mental framing techniques are shared with the group to help them think about what they think about. By recognizing one's current mindset, it's easier to elevate to a more innovative one.

Participants are again shown the picture. Like turning on a light, creativity fills the room as they imagine the picture in new ways and empathize with what it represents. This thinking allows them to do what they couldn't do previously. By burning new neuropaths through conscious thought and vivid imagining, they see potential for a new reality — and their actions follow.

Now picture a pathway that is worn, potholed, and somewhat unkept. This is a mindset that defaults to routine, deflective, or mimic responses. Full of potential, it's underutilized and not well tended. Circumstance and fear steal more than their share of mental real estate. Rote reactions displace intentionality — especially when the stakes are high or opportunities new. And, innovation stops before it could begin.

All else equal, positioning your thinking for the *possibility* of identifying valuable innovation provides at least two benefits. First, it better predicts that you'll take that path because you've actively invested in creating it. Just as magnets attract metal, certain patterns of thought entice doing. An innovative mindset didn't casually nudge Jeff Bezos towards Amazon's founding ideas. He anchored his thoughts towards growth possibilities, which broadened his capacity to uncover valuable innovation. And, he had the audacity to act.

Second, because thinking and doing travel a related mental road, what you envision tends to shape your results.[29][30][31]

The path to valuable innovation is littered with real and perceived obstacles. Effective Bridgers mentally remove the obstacles they can control to focus their effort and resources on other obstacles that new innovations tend to confront.

DESIRES AND ACTIONS

An adapted experiment from a science center in San Francisco highlights the importance of mentally removing controllable obstacles.

The simulation takes place in two stages. First, participants are positioned about three meters from a board about the size of 72' inch television perched atop a sturdy post — as if nearly free-stranding in place. Participants are instructed that one side of the board is painted a darker shade of gray than the other. This is obviously the case to observers.

The participant is then blindfolded and spun in a circle. The board is also spun in a circle like a pinwheel. When both stop spinning, and with the participant still blindfolded, a large tassel (a bunch of cords fixed together to cover anything in its path) is placed down the center of the board — hiding the dividing line between the two painted sides.

Blindfold removed but tassel in place, the participant is asked to determine the side painted the darker shade of gray.

---

29   Hunsaker, B.T. (2019) Mindset Positioning: Premier Development Edition.

30   Jenkins, A. C., Dodell-Feder, D., Saxe, R., & Knobe, J. (2014). The Neural Bases of Directed and Spontaneous Mental State Attributions to Group Agents. *PloS one*, 9(8), e105341.

31   Carter, C (2014) Greater Good Center. UC-Berkeley.

Figure 1 includes a recreation of the experiment with either side of the image featuring a darker and lighter shade of gray, and the connecting line covered.

Figure 1   **Blinding Tassel**

Tassel in place, participants are reduced to guessing. It's nearly impossible to determine the darker shade of gray. Invariably the participant and onlookers reach for "trick-of-hand" explanations. "You switched the board while I was blindfolded" and "they're now the same" are the most common.

There is no "trick-of-hand" deception.

To prove this, the experiment operator removes the tassel to reveal that one side is, in fact, painted a darker shade of gray. Figure 2 contains a recreation of the board with the tassel removed. Interesting as a science experiment, the implications are even richer with mindset's influence on innovation in focus.

Consider what this tassel represents to the would-be innovator. In place, an otherwise straightforward determination is almost impossible. Removed, line of sight becomes clear. And, in nearly all cases the tassels are largely self-imposed.

Figure 2 **Blinding Tassel Revealed**

Analyzing thousands of managers, the most common self-imposed mental *tassels* emerge.

HURDLING LEGITIMACY ROADBLOCKS

Overwhelmingly, surveyed managers express that they want to be innovative. In nearly equal numbers, however, those same managers don't want to be the first to stand out. The latter can't exist without the former, so just as a small spark without fuel struggles to produce a flame, innovation tends to stop in the mind.

The desire to look and feel and act like others is strong. With good reason. Conformity tends to make the individual and the surrounding group comfortable with each other. But comfort rarely produces innovation.

Greek philosopher Plato's axiom for this dilemma is instructive, "wise men speak because they have something to say; fools because they have to say something."[32]

---

32   Cooper, J. M., & Hutchinson, D. S. (Eds.). (1997). *Plato: complete works.* Hackett Publishing.

Having to say something is largely a function of trying to gain legitimacy by mirroring the crowd. Whereas, having something to say tends to result from willingness to consider the benefits of a norm's counterpoint or an altogether new thought.

To be sure, conformity has its place. But ordering matters. Most useful in the implementation of ideas, once a great innovation has been identified, vetted, and needs to be proliferated, it too often acts as the mind's gatekeeper at the beginning of a process and crowds out new ideas altogether. As Plato also observed, "the beginning is the most important part of the work."[33] Willingness to be open to the possibility for innovation, and courage to serve as its scout or author, is key.

SCRAPPINESS AS A VIRTUE

The second common mental tassel is sluffing ideas for fear of what they'll require. Successful innovators find virtue in the scrappiness needed to get new ideas off the ground. Others convince themselves it's not worth it.

In a sub-set of the managers surveyed, most projected they'd had what they thought to be a great idea in the previous year. Fewer than half took any action to further explore or validate the idea — let alone the heavier lifting of making it reality. In follow up interviews that allowed for more interaction and context, overwhelmingly these managers did not want to sign up for the work they knew sponsoring new ideas would take. So, they resisted. Over time this became easier — until they rarely scouted new ideas at all.

PULL OF THE PRIOR

While Wall Street is largely built on using prior performance to sell equities, prior experience can be a significant mental impediment to innovation. This is especially the case when dealing with sunk costs (an expense that's already occurred and can't be recovered).

---

33   Cooper, J. M., & Hutchinson, D. S. (Eds.). (1997). Plato: complete works. Hackett Publishing.

Ideas that run counter to the manager's sunk costs are quickly and almost universally dismissed, based on a study of nearly 100 managers by researchers at the Thunderbird School of Global Management. Less expected, however, is just how powerful this force is at the more benign level of ideas that simply seek to improve upon the sunk cost. These, too, were dismissed at nearly a 70% rate without further inquiry.

To be sure, effectively harnessed previous experience can be a valuable launchpad to subsequent learning and discovery. Prior thinking can also be a strong obstruction to future growth without techniques to combat this tendency.

MINDSET & ACTION SET

Arranging your thoughts to invite the possibility that a great idea is around the corner, and you can be the conduit for it, ignites a series of physiological responses that impact emotional attitudes — where activity quality is largely influenced. That's why talented people can underwhelm despite clear relative superiority, and others can shape their thinking to kindle a positive response regardless of circumstance.

This isn't unlike the findings of researchers at Cal-Berkeley who asked, *do we smile instinctively because we're happy or does the act of smiling contribute to our happiness?* They found significant support for the latter.

— When you paste on a smile there is something at work that is pretty amazing: facial expressions themselves can actually make us feel. If you wrinkle your nose and narrow your eyes as you would if you were really angry, your body will release some adrenaline and your heart rate may speed up as if you were actually angry. The same thing is true for other emotions. This means that sometimes we should just smile, even if we don't feel like it. As horribly forced as that sounds, there is solid science to back up the notion that this will, in fact, make us feel happier.[34]

Replace smiling with certain patterns of thought and happiness with other purposeful attitudes and a similar effect emerges.

---

34   Carter, C. (2009, 2014). http://greatergood.berkeley.edu/raising_happiness/post/fake_it_till_you_make_it. Retrieved September 2, 2015.

This is where fear, which tends to stifle venturing, obligation, which completes tasks out of duty but fails to embrace their potential, or hope born of 'get to' appreciation and 'what could be' bullishness tends to take hold and either derail innovation-generating actions before they take root or provide the fertile soil for seeking valuable ideas,

First, win within isn't the end game but the precursor to winning the broader game. Without it, no amount of technical savvy will produce the desired innovation results. Combined with key techniques, however, repeatable game-changer innovation is within reach to all.

Discovery section →

Part I: Respond

Respond to the questions below using the following rating scale:
A = Always.   B = Often.   C = Sometimes.   D = Rarely.   E = Never.

10. My innovation effort matches
    my desires

11. I stand out from the crowd for things
    I believe in

12. Previous experience informs me, but
    doesn't govern me

13. I'm willing to do the work needed to advance
    an idea

Part II: Describe

For the following questions, describe what first comes to mind. **Don't** state what you think you should say, but rather what best represents your experience.

A) Think of a recent scenario when you had the opportunity to stand out from the crowd. Did you seize it? Why or why not?

B) Think of someone you would consider scrappy. What is your impression of this characteristic — both positive and negative?

Suggested responses to Part I: D, A, A, A

C) Think of a scenario when you thought you should change, but had much invested in the current course. What did you do? Why?

_____

_____

_____

_____

_____

Given what you now know after reading this chapter, and upon further reflection, when in similar scenarios in the future HOW YOU WOULD LIKE TO RESPOND?

A)

_____

_____

_____

_____

_____

B)

_____

_____

_____

_____

_____

_____

c)

_____

_____

_____

_____

_____

_____

_____

Practice Activities Section

Compare two scenarios from your recent experiences involving winning within — one more and one less successful. What did you think about prior to the outcome? How prevalent was your sense of gratitude? How did your mindset possibly influence the result?

■ Experience #1 — More Successful

_____

_____

_____

_____

■ Experience #2 — Less Successful

_____

_____

_____

_____

_____

Given a similar scenario going forward, how could you build from the more successful elements and improve on the less successful ones?

The value of an insight is found in its doing. What are at least two concrete actions that can help you to more consistently "First, Win Within?"

_____

_____

_____

_____

_____

_____

_____

_____

_____

What benefit(s) do you anticipate from doing these actions well?

_____

_____

_____

_____

_____

_____

_____

_____

_____

_____

_____

_____

_____

_____

BUILD
A BIGGER BOX

A sked to 'think outside the box,' attendees of an innovation workshop nodded at the familiar suggestion. But within the time allotted they struggled to produce meaningful ideas. Though common jargon — this prompt provides little useful guidance to how great ideas are developed.

To get the most out of your efforts start by *building a bigger box.* This recommendation is a variation on 'think outside the box.' The human mind is wired to make sense of its surroundings through conceptual frameworks, or 'boxes,' — thinking is always aided by boundaries. Instead of telling people to think outside the box (which can result in disconnected and unrealistic ideas — and isn't neurologically natural), a more useful ideation approach is to expand the box.

Building a bigger box means that you recognize that products and services are not simply exchanged — they become ongoing relationships. You don't just buy sticky notes; you take them home and use them over an extended period. If you are focused just on the moments that directly surround the purchase, you are missing most of the relationship. What prompts a customer to buy these sticky notes? What is her ongoing experience like? When you observe customers, recognize that you are only observing a small fraction of the full relationship and your job is to try and get at the entire relationship and relevant industry dynamics. You need to consider what happens before and after.

An example from the owner of a fast-casual restaurant illustrates this recommendation. She wanted to identify new ideas that could take her business to the next level, so she began doing what most people would naturally do. She started by thinking about what was happening inside her building. She observed the customers; they enjoyed the food (they made positive comments and demonstrated visible enjoyment). They seemed content with the tidy environment and the service. She did notice that her food was messy and customers used a lot of napkins. So, she started ordering larger, higher quality napkins as a way to increase customer satisfaction — but this was a very incremental idea.

She was then prompted to expand the box — to think about what is going on *before* the customer arrives and what happens *after* the customer leaves (this is a way to see the whole picture and to understand insertion in the value chain). She began by asking customers at what point during the day did they decide to come to the restaurant. She discovered that many customers wanted to come much more frequently, but it was just too far for them to drive. This led to other questions and observations and she finally decided to open a mobile food truck (to supplement the store). Eventually she expanded to a dozen trucks. Her monthly revenue increased and her monthly profits climbed (lower overhead costs of the trucks made them much more profitable than the original restaurant location). By considering what was happening before her customers arrived, she was able to identify a great idea that dramatically grew her business.

Looking at what happens before an exchange prompts you to think about who opted out of the experience before it occurred. Looking at what happens after the exchange can help you understand why a customer may drop out of the relationship. If you are only focusing on the exchange snapshot, you will miss this type of information.

When Howard Schultz' started observing Italians in the espresso bar, he was observing a group of non-customers. He realized that these were people who would never be Starbucks' customers if the company clung to their 'brew-at-home' model. The insight he developed would never have happened if he had been wedded to only looking inside the overly narrow view of his current customers. It was by expanding the box to include non-customers, that he was able to generate a great idea that transformed the coffee industry.

ESSENCE

The most valuable ideas are not found in common surface events, but in seeing and translating their underlying conditions. Whether directly observed in interpersonal exchanges or packaged as social events or industry trends across time, all human experiences emit functional, emotional and psychological cues that signal whether value is gained or lost in a given scenario. The ability to infer sources of friction or satisfaction, displeasure or joy within the bigger box is fundamental to finding great ideas. A uniquely human capability, this cannot be easily substituted by technology or statistical analysis so it is vital that you become skilled at seeking and translating these cues.

Most people are able to move in this direction — they can more consciously observe underlying implications — but doing so requires focused effort. An activity designed for and used with over 1,000 managers from dozens of countries demonstrates the difference. Managers are divided into two representative groups. One group is shown a video of department-store shoppers and asked to write down their observations. The other group is shown the same video and given the same amount of time to record their observations, but prior to watching the video they are prompted to consider satisfaction and dissatisfaction — what people really care about in the exchange–exhibited by the people in the video.

The managers who are provided the prompt make much more valuable observations when watching the video. They notice the shoppers who are stuck in traffic bottlenecks, having difficulty finding desired products, unfamiliar with the store layout, or unable to find the dressing room—all potential seeds of store innovation. They empathize with the frustrations those scenarios represent and start to think of ways to improve them. Those without the prompt tend to focus on surface events and extraneous details—the color of a shopper's shirt, the type of food on the shelves, the brightness of the store's lights — none being particularly noteworthy. Importantly, surface observations occur repeatedly only in the groups that aren't provided the prompt.

This experiment highlights that finding great ideas is not DNA dependent. Despite differences in socio-economic status, gender, upbringing, language, and country of origin the only significant factor in participants' ability to intelligently decipher was whether they received and heeded a simple prompt when viewing the video. Looking at events this way transforms otherwise scattered, surface events into a purposeful search for opportunity.

The human mechanism to express pleasure or pain is through emotion. Every experience emits a story. And, effective discovery and observation unpack these stories. Getting to the story's essence–why interest or satisfaction rises or falls — is vital to sensing drivers of value.

You can lie to yourself if you fail to observe the emotion and psychology associated with your enterprise. Without careful observation, for example, you can invent theories for why someone loves your product or one you're analyzing. Prior to Netflix's initial rise, we spoke with a Blockbuster employee who believed that Netflix wasn't a threat because people loved going to Blockbuster on a Friday night, browsing the rows for a video — this was an 'experience' that customers enjoyed. When we pressed and asked him to really observe how people were feeling and thinking, he came back with a very different story. He saw a high number of customers leaving the store frustrated and this opened his eyes to the threat that Netflix really posed.

There are three ways to observe any event. The surface level, or level1, entails passively consuming information with limited consideration. Like casually watching a television program in a desensitized state, the environment is simply scanned without regard to understanding what may be causing events to unfold. This level is casual in nature and almost never produces great ideas.

At level 2, the most common destination for observations, assumptions about what is causing the events are formed and provide the basis for interpreting them. You see something happen and quickly categorize and assign it value based on your existing concept of what is right and wrong. As with the common practice of pseudo-listening (listening in a distracted way or with a hidden agenda), you can instinctively filter out what you do not agree with and emphasize what you do.

Preconceived ideas are projected onto the environment rather than allowing the environment to unveil new ones–molding information to meet an existing ideal rather than openly learning from the information. Observed behaviors are judged rather than genuinely considered. Assumptions, rather than questions, fill information gaps. And the dominant story line is not what the actors in the scene portray they really care about, but rather what you think they *should* care about. The danger at this level is often the most valuable ideas are packaged as paradoxes — or occurrences contrary to expectations — which a strictly evaluative approach is likely to veil.

Level 3 entails authentically inferring the functional, emotional and psychological cues expressed in given scenarios without initially judging them. This does not have to take a lot of time, but it does require conscious effort. While engaging the environment, it can be easy to assume new observations are inferior to or incompatible with what is already known. This is tempered by the motive to learn — a genuine curiosity. Statements like, "that's odd" or "that doesn't make sense" or "they should just do it this way" give way to, "I wonder what's causing her to do that?" and "what do people care about most in this situation?" and "what's the gap between what is available and what people really care about?" These questions invite consideration for what is important. At this level, the cues start to form meaningful windows into what people really care about — and how this is and is not met by their current reality.

When Howard Shultz of Starbucks went to Milan, he spent time observing the espresso café scene, but more importantly he determined to understand what made it vibrant. He revisited places that stood out as unique and spent time considering what made them so. While simple in deed, this act proved profound in gesture because it prompted him to uncover the essence of what was valuable in the espresso café experience, he observed. As valuable cues are noted, the next step in a level 3 is to ask, 'why is this occurring?'

Participants prompted to look for underlying intent in the shopping video experiment start to attach psychological meaning to the images before them. They convert still images to animations and begin to see through participant eyes. Rather than skimming the surface, they interact with the images and empathize those inside to identify important cues and then ask why the people in the video are experiencing the cues they are exhibiting — giving the cues meaning. What is she doing? Why is she doing it that way? Is it causing joy or dissatisfaction? What about the person's environment is contributing to the cues being transmitted? Are these cues unique or generalizable to others?

Each cue has underlying meaning. Asking 'why' helps pinpoint the source of the cues and to more accurately build their underlying story. Rather than assume causality, you are driven to engage in rich, meaningful dialogue with the cues to consider what about a particular event, exchange or scenario is motiving the responses conveyed.

Great ideas rarely beg to be noticed. They must be uncovered. Schultz could have taken the more common approach and determined that what he saw was uniquely Italian and wasn't applicable to other communities. He could have projected biases related to the amount of time wasted as people interacted in the cafes. He could have discounted his observations as inferior to prevailing business models or assumed they weren't relevant because someone else hadn't already implemented them. Any one of these conclusions would have prompted him to dismiss what he observed as incompatible with his existing sense of reality and derailed his ability to find a great idea — just as hundreds of other coffee executives had done before him.

But he didn't.

Instead, he paused and he watched. He listened. As verbal and non-verbal cues directed, he took note of the emotional value derived from embedding coffee into socially appealing activities — something completely counter to the commodity driven model that then dominated the industry. This prompted him to dig deeper. And to see value that others missed. The result is one of the great stories of modern business.[35][36][37][38]

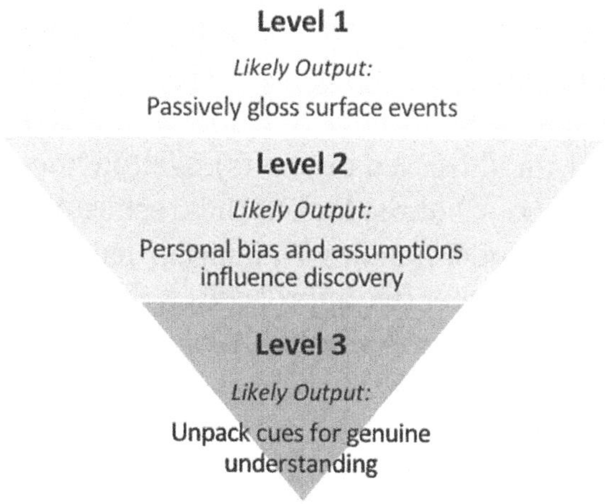

Level 1

Likely Output:
Passively gloss surface events

Level 2

Likely Output:
Personal bias and assumptions
influence discovery

Level 3

Likely Output:
Unpack cues for genuine
understanding

Figure 3 **Observation Levels**

---

35 Leavy, B. (2016). Effective leadership today–character not just competence. *Strategy & Leadership*.

36 Simmons, J. (2012). *The Starbucks story: how the brand changed the world.* Marshall Cavendish International Asia Pte Ltd.

37 Schultz, H., & Gordon, J. (2012). Onward: *How Starbucks fought for its life without losing its soul.* Rodale books.

38 Koehn, N. F. (2001). Howard Schultz and Starbucks coffee company.

INTELLIGENTLY DECIPHER

Noticing something is different from understanding its value. Building a bigger box expands your temporal view of the customer experience by considering the before, during, and after experience, while deciphering helps you to make sense of what matters most in this expanded view. This involves understanding an activity's impact on people's lives.

An effective way to do this is to unbundle the experience into its various pieces and consider what about the experience customers *like*, what they *don't like* and their potential causes (such as bureaucratic process or layers or firm rigidity), and what evokes *ambivalence*. Areas they *like* are opportunities for further investment, areas of *ambivalence* absorb resources that are better redirected (often an overlooked source of funding for new ideas), and areas they *don't like* represent disruptive terrain requiring reinvention or reimagination (e.g. inconvenience, price, misfit functionality, service friction, low optimization that could be automated, unaddressed interests). Walton knew his customers liked low prices, but the lack of the freshest items often sent them elsewhere. Understanding Walmart's then disruptive terrain, combined with the other two approaches we've mentioned, helped Walton to quickly recognize a system's value that could consistently deliver speed and freshness to consumers.

While building a bigger box is about seeing the bigger picture, intelligently deciphering creates depth in your understanding of the customer experience and begins to distinguish valuable observations.

It is helpful to recognize that the customer experience is a bundle — and you will get a better profile of the customer if you disaggregate this bundle. For example, when Netflix founder Reed Hastings initially considered the movie rental industry, it was useful for him to think about the experience in *before, during,* and *after* segments — customers decided they needed a video, they had to go to the store and select a video, they waited in line to rent the video, they took the video home and watched it; they returned the video. Considering how customers felt (*like, dislike, ambivalence*) about different pieces of that experience provided key insights to launch Netflix.[39][40][41][42]

The tool in Figure 4 combines the key elements to building a bigger box in a single framework.

Better observations will consider the before, during, and after experience and categorize what is liked, disliked, or met with ambivalence at each stage. Elements that are liked could be carried forward in the new idea or considered for additional investment. Disliked elements represent the most fertile ground for disruption (often among the more difficult things to admit about our own offerings — making doing so the more vital).

For incumbents, this is critical to ongoing innovation efforts. For new entrants, this provides clues for where to focus disruption resources. In either case, identifying points of ambivalence allows you to remove or shift these elements from the offering and redirect these resources to bolster like and help fund dislike items.

Customer Experience	Like (protect, nurture, expand)	Dislike (reimagine, disrupt)	Ambivalent (redirect resources)
Before			
During			
After			

Figure 4   **Bigger Box Grid**

---

39   Rataul, P., Tisch, D. G., & Zámborský, P. (2018). Netflix: Dynamic capabilities for global success. SAGE Publications: SAGE Business Cases Originals.

40   HENRY, C. (2018). LEADERSHIP AND STRATEGY IN THE NEWS. *STRATEGY & LEADERSHIP.*

41   Grinapol, C. (2013). *Reed Hastings and Netflix.* The Rosen Publishing Group, Inc.

42   Farrow, R. (2012). Netflix heads into the clouds.
Discovery section →

Part I: Respond

Respond to the questions below using the following rating scale:
A = Always.   B = Often.   C = Sometimes.   D = Rarely.   E = Never.

14. When in a new situation, I quickly compare it to my own experience and make a judgement about its value?

15. Others close to me say I ask great questions before thinking I have the answer?

16. I create opportunities for others to share what they don't like about the experience I'm providing?

Part II: Describe

For the following questions, describe how you would most likely respond. To get the most from your efforts, **don't** describe what you *think you should do*, but rather *what you would most likely actually do* based on how you've responded to similar situations in the past.

You're given the challenge to come up with a new idea. How would you do this?

Suggested responses to Part I D, A, A

How would you like your innovation approach to improve for having reviewed this chapter's insights? If you were asked to explain to others how to "Build a Bigger Box," what would you share?

Practice Activities Section

Choose an experience you'd like to consider for its innovation opportunities. This can be from your current work or another aspect of life. For example, if you work in the medical industry you may consider the patient visit experience.

Step #1 — What are key elements in the Before, During, and After experience?

Before _____

_____

_____

_____

_____

During _____

_____

_____

_____

_____

After _____

_____

_____

_____

_____

_____

DISCOVERY SECTION

Step #2 — What is Liked, Disliked, and a source of Ambivalence in each element?

LIKE

Before

During

After

DISLIKE

Before

During

After

AMBIVALENCE

Before

During

After

The value of an insight is found in its doing. What are at least two concrete actions that can help you to more consistently "Build a Bigger Box?"

What benefit(s) do you anticipate from doing these actions well?

CONNECT
THE OPPORTUNITY

Building a bigger box helps Bridgers to focus their observations and understand the total customer experience in a given industry or segment of that industry. Sources of friction, unmet interests, and sub-optimization are identified. To become durable advantages, these gaps (problems to be solved within the experience) must be turned into future-oriented, valuably better solutions.

Disciplined observation will also surface experience elements customers hold dear. These should be retained, albeit improved, in the future offering. By isolating what is disliked (gaps; problems to be solved) and liked (elements to be carried forward) in an industry's current approach, and the related customer experience, the foundation is in place to consider how to change the experience for good — to connect the opportunity. What follows is a focused design question that centers on connecting the opportunity to a potential solution.

Consider the example of Amazon entering new sales modalities. Retail shopping models had long been considered binary–either e-commerce or brick and mortar. In practice the industry involved a long spectrum with pure e-commerce on one end and pure brick and mortar on the other end. In between, many different models were emerging like ordering online and picking up in-store (Walmart's Grocery Pickup[43]), shopping in-store and ordering online (Warby Parker[44] and Bonobos[45] made their name in this space — largely facilitating the showroom behavior of consumers), digitally-enhanced physical shopping (several companies hold patents in this space with virtual reality promising to push this model), and many others.

By 2019 Amazon, was the world's most valuable online retailer exceeding $1 trillion (USD).[46] So, when the company announced the purchase of Whole Foods and further committed to the expansion of Amazon Go store locations many questioned the opportunity.[47] Why would a company so clearly successful in the digital realm seek to enter the more traditional brick and mortar space?

Despite Amazon's online retailing success, the company depended largely on a single modality that constrained the overall customer experience and potentially limited growth. For example, some existing and potential customers liked to hold a physical book before buying it. Others were not comfortable with packages being left at unsecured doorsteps. Home security videos of package-grabbers appeared frequently on social media, especially during holiday seasons. Additionally, while some items, like food, could be delivered to homes, many customers liked the option of being able to touch and smell their fresh produce before buying it.

Amazon Go, founded in 2018, reimagined the convenience-store customer-buying experience in altogether new ways by introducing physical stores with self-serve virtual check out. Employing *Just*

---

43   https://www.sec.gov/Archives/edgar/data/1018724/000119312507093886/dex991. htm. Retrieved 12 May 2019 https://www.produceretailer.com/article/news-article/ walmart-snagging-these-shoppers-grocery-pickup

44   https://www.warbyparker.com/. Retrieved June 4, 2019.

45   https://bonobos.com/ Retrieved June 7, 2019

46   NASDAQ: AMZN. Retrieved May 14, 2019.

47   wholefoodsmarket.com/news/amazon-and-whole-foods-market-announce-acquisition-to-close-this-monday-wil. Retrieved January 10, 2019.

Walk Out Shopping Technology, Amazon Go introduced customers to the ability to completely bypass checkout lines. A team of Amazon executives tested the Go store concept in a 15,000-square-foot mock supermarket in a converted rented warehouse in Seattle. They then introduced the idea to Amazon founder Jeff Bezos in 2015. The first real Go store, open only to employees as of December 2016, provided opportunities to test and debug the Go store model. Amazon did not open the store until January 2018. The announcement of the first store opening led to a 2.5% jump in Amazon's stock price. This change increased Jeff Bezos' net worth by $2.8 billion in a single day.[48]

Bezos commented, "With Amazon Go, we had a clear vision. Get rid of the worst thing about physical retail: checkout lines. No one likes to wait in line. Instead, we imagined a store where you could walk in, pick up what you wanted, and leave."[49] To achieve this goal would require significant fusion of technological capabilities, including computer vision, AI deep learning algorithms, and sensor fusion solutions to achieve the level of automation required for self-service checkout that would be secure for both customers and the company. Sensor fusion combined data from cameras and scales and bar codes to verify purchases. Amazon developers created the Amazon Go app for iOS and Android mobile devices. The app served as the primary payment method. It was easy for app users to add family members to their account so they could make purchases.

One industry analyst for RBC Wealth Management described Amazon Go as "Almost like the experience of shoplifting, except it's legal, and you don't need to hide the stuff in your jacket...Its in-store technology enables shoppers to have a very efficient and

48 https://www.investopedia.com/news/jeff-bezos-just-got-28-billion-richer-thanks-amazon-go/ Retrieved December 10, 2019.

49 https://www.cnbc.com/2019/04/12/amazons-jeff-bezos-most-us-sales-still-in-brick-and-mortar-stores.html Retrieved December 2, 2019

pleasant shopping experience. The overall opportunity is huge."[50] By Spring 2019, the company had 18 Go store locations in Seattle, Chicago, San Francisco, and New York City.

Bezos and Amazon precisely embodied the Bridger method when they introduced storefronts with self-serve virtual check-outs. Their previous, digitally-exclusive model left many customers wanting for a tangible store experience. And, most consumers of in-person retail shared a dislike for waiting in lines. In both experiences, customers cared about value-driven pricing and selection — both elements Amazon would not want to alienate in the new experience.

With observations derived from building-a-bigger-box developed, it's helpful to frame an opportunity question. Questions invoke openness in ways statements can't. For example, the simultaneously vague and confining "we need a better solution" becomes "how can we deepen what's liked in the experience and reimagine what's not?"

The opportunity question for Amazon could have read:

— How can we provide a physical shopping experience that leverages our digital, pricing, and selection capabilities while eliminating waiting in line?

OBSERVATION TO OPPORTUNITY

If building a bigger box focuses scouting efforts on assessing likes, dislikes, and ambivalence in an industry or customer experience — similar to surfacing the key pieces to a puzzle — turning these observations into potentially beneficial change gives them their value. Identifying the need is part of the equation. Fitting observation to opportunity follows.

Three considerations and their tools aid this process.

1. Shaping Forces Visualization
2. Inefficient Monetization & Rent Pockets
3. Persona Mapping

---

50   https://www.forbes.com/sites/andriacheng/2019/01/13/why-amazon-go-may-soon-change-the-way-we-want-to- shop/#4dbc86a76709. Retrieved May 26, 2019.

SHAPING FORCES VISUALIZATION

Winston Churchill's quote during his 1948 speech to the House of Commons, "Those who fail to learn from history are doomed to repeat it" is nimbler than even the pithy Churchill may have intended. And, learning from history is not confined to just one context.

Take Kublai Khan's lost fleet during the attempted attack on Japan in 1274. A rebuilt fleet suffered the same fate in 1291, killing tens of thousands of troops across the two events.

Similarly, the Spanish Armada fleet of 130 ships on a 16th century mission to invade England was thwarted by heavy storms, despite significant advancement in ship technology. Nearly 5000 soldiers lost their lives as their vessels slammed against the Scottish and Irish coastlines.

Across the centuries thousands of ships have ventured into open waters and, despite progressively fantastic engineering, lost the battle with a storm-powered sea. In the 21st century, alone, hundreds of thousands of lives have been lost when even the most advanced ships went head-to-head with a raging ocean.

This part of history's lesson is clear: great ideas and shaping forces, working together rather than apart, present the best opportunities.

Forces that mandate expenditures in value-chains (activities firms engage to deliver a product or service to market) or shape how a service must operate are high in *requirement* and are most congruent with opportunities focused on cost, convenience, and reliability. For example, auto insurance would likely have far less market traction if it weren't required by law. Few consumers find this segment interesting, but rather an obligation. They are looking to meet the requirement as seamlessly as possible and to receive quality service in the unfortunate event of an auto accident. For this segment, solution ideas that work with this shaping force and focus on reducing consumer costs, improving purchase and user convenience, and enhancing reliability are more likely to present advantageous opportunities.

A skilled Bridger may observe that people *like* limited but reliable interaction with their insurance company, *dislike* having to call for quote updates, and care little about the in-office agent experience. There are strong foreseeable forces to support the trend for requiring insurance for all vehicles, so the opportunity domain is turning these observations into a more a cost-effective, convenient, and reliable consumer experience.

Contrast this with low-requirement, but high-interest forces. These are largely socially-oriented and tend to focus on status. There is no law requiring a fashionable purse, and no functional explanation for its purchase beyond the cost to make it, but several brands command thousands of dollars per item.[51][52][53][54]

When the force assessment is *interesting* high, but *required* low the primary opportunity dimensions are quality, choice, and status. Savvy marketing and education will be key to highlight distinctive qualities and to build and expand desired followership. Potential solutions that focus on these dimensions tend to represent better fit-to-purpose opportunities in this shaping force environment.

In some cases, forces align and are highly required *and* interesting. Many forms of employment require smart phones. So do many forms of social engagement. In these cases, the opportunity dimension blend is better seized by solution ideas that fuse quality and status. Conversely, the lack of both *required* and *interesting* forces signal that better opportunity resides elsewhere. In all cases, effective Bridgers assess forces to understand opportunity trends — congruently pursuing those that are expanding.

51   Showrav, D., & Nitu, R. (2018). The influence of brand equity on customer intention to pay premium price of the fashion house brand. *Management Science Letters, 8*(12), 1291-1304.

52   Bıçakcıoğlu, N., Ögel, İ. Y., & İlter, B. (2017). Brand jealousy and willingness to pay premium: The mediating role of materialism. *Journal of brand Management, 24*(1), 33-48.

53   Li, G., Li, G., & Kambele, Z. (2012). Luxury fashion brand consumers in China: Perceived value, fashion lifestyle, and willingness to pay. *Journal of Business Research, 65*(10), 1516-1522.

54   Katz, J. E., & Sugiyama, S. (2006). Mobile phones as fashion statements: evidence from student surveys in the US and Japan. *New media & society, 8*(2), 321-337.

Ideas void of required or behavioral interest shaping forces alert effective Bridgers to seek opportunity elsewhere.

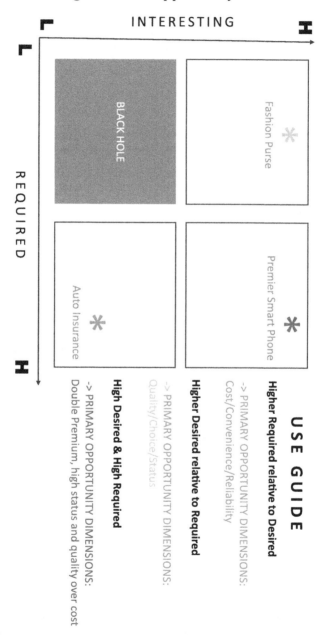

Figure 5 **Shaping Forces Visualization Tool**

INEFFICIENT MONETIZATION & RENT POCKETS

In economics, *rents* are an amount of money earned that exceeds what is economically or socially necessary.[55][56][57] In the positive, this explains that some goods and services can attract premium margins beyond what perfect competition would produce. But rents can also represent sub-optimization that is prime for disruption. This form often results from resource scarcity, policy rather than market-driven funding, or limited competition.

Rents, in many ways, are inefficiently monetized relationships in which the over or under supply of capital skews the cost of goods. For example, the US government's enormous defense budget for decades attracted interest from enterprising firms but also yielded many examples of overpriced goods. While there are short-sighted returns for rent seekers, in the globally connected, digital era the greater opportunity is in rent disrupting — targeting value chain activities that are important but sub-optimized.

Inefficiently monetized but important relationships and sizeable rent pockets, reconsidered, signal potential for uncommonly valuable opportunities that can likely scale.

Think of the imbalance between the supply of global entrepreneurs and the concentration of global capital. Entrepreneurs need capital to grow their enterprises. Global capital needs quality deal flow to earn attractive returns. Yet, like a bottlenecked hourglass, both parties believe there's not enough of the other. This is an example of *bigger-box* observations about an industry surfacing the potential for tremendous opportunity through disrupting a rent pock by driving access and scale efficiency into the global entrepreneur/global capital relationship.

---

55 Caballero, R. J., Farhi, E., & Gourinchas, P. O. (2017). Rents, technical change, and risk premia accounting for secular trends in interest rates, returns on capital, earning yields, and factor shares. *American Economic Review, 107*(5), 614-20.

56 Tomaskovic-Devey, D., & Lin, K. H. (2011). Income dynamics, economic rents, and the financialization of the US economy. *American Sociological Review, 76*(4), 538-559.

57 Lado, A. A., Boyd, N. G., & Hanlon, S. C. (1997). Competition, cooperation, and the search for economic rents: A syncretic model. *Academy of management review, 22*(1), 110-141.

Figure 6   **Disrupting Inefficient Monetization &/Or Reconsidering Rent Pockets**

Identify inefficiently monetized relationships where rents are accumulating, and:
Seek *like* compatibility points to leverage and change the *dislike* interaction elements

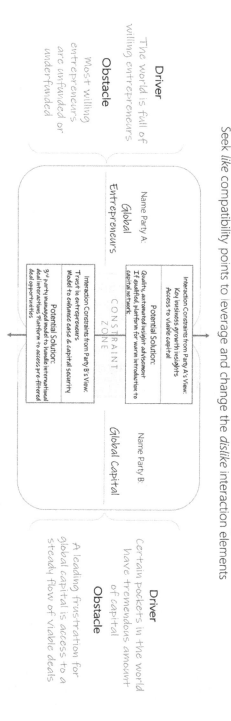

Driver

The world is full of
willing entrepreneurs

Obstacle

Most willing
entrepreneurs
are unfunded or
underfunded

**Global
Entrepreneurs**

Name Party A:

Interaction Constraints from Party A's View:
Key business growth insights
Access to viable capital

Potential Solution:
Quality, automated insight advisement
If qualified, platform for warm introduction to
capital network.

CONSTRAINT
ZONE

Name Party B:

Interaction Constraints from Party B's View:
Trust in entrepreneurs
Model to enhance ease & capital security

Potential Solution:
3rd party managed model to handle international
deal interactions. Platform to access pre-filtered
deal opportunities

Global Capital

Driver

Certain pockets in the world
have tremendous amount
of capital

Obstacle

A leading frustration for
global capital is access to a
steady flow of viable deals

91

PERSONA MAPPING

As observations and opportunities begin to connect, honing in on the intended audience is key. Opportunity-relevant scale is most desired, but rather than trying to serve 'everyone' all successful ventures serve a specific 'someone.'

The Persona Canvas (Exhibit 7) helps users to consider *bigger-box* observations and opportunity statements for particular audiences. Industry observations open would-be innovators to possibilities by broadly surfacing the likes, dislikes, and ambivalence in a given experience, but shaping the future by mapping those efforts to actionable opportunities requires identifying a core audience.

Focusing on a target customer does not mean others are not welcome to buy from you or are uncared for. It does mean that these other groups are not your *core*, so you should focus your attention on who can and should be your central target and focus on them with precision.

Major Australian hardware chain, Bunnings, discovered this when they entered the UK market with disastrous results. The same thing that served them so well in Australia, a laser-clear sense for their target audience (male do-it-yourself project patrons), betrayed them when they acquired UK company Homebase with the intent to convert their stores to the Bunnings model. The problem was Homebase's core customer was a 'female home and garden enhancer.' When Bunnings approached Homebased customers with their Australian target customer in mind they failed and were abruptly forced to exit the market.[58]

Knowing your core audience, and placing all others in the periphery, injects opportunity framing efforts with discipline and focus that, ultimately, increase success odds.

---

58 https://www.smh.com.au/business/companies/going-off-script-how-the-1-7b-bunnings-uk-disaster-unfolded-20180528-p4zhvw.html. Retrieved March 3, 2020.

Figure 7 **Persona Canvas**

Age:
Sex:
Location:
Income:
Edu:

What they *dislike* about the experience:

What they *like* about the experience:

What they're *ambivalent* to about the experience:

What They Want	What They Want to Avoid	Causes & Values	Ability & Willingness to Pay

How can we provide X (proposed solution to DISLIKED elements) _____

To Y (target audience) _____

While preserving or improving Z (LIKED ELEMENTS) _____

WRITE YOUR SOLUTION HYPOTHESIS

All of your efforts to understand the customer experience and related industry dynamics will only matter if you turn this insight into a coherent statement about how to valuably enhance the customer experience. Writing a formal hypothesis (a tentative and testable working statement about the customer experience) helps you to distill your ideas to their most important parts and to consider how your idea is expected to influence your business model or produce a new one. A strong hypothesis is grounded in the proposed solution and its intended outcome. Taking this action prompts you to objectively refine and validate ideas.

A well-constructed hypothesis is a testable expression of cause and effect ("If X (the idea), then Y (anticipated outcome"). It doesn't need to be longer than a sentence and should target the core challenge to be solved.

For example, Starbuck's Howard Schultz could have come up with the following: *If coffee is served in a vibrant social setting then coffee drinkers would be willing to pay more for it.*

The initial idea to be tested was to turn a commoditizing item into a vibrant social and status-oriented experience. With this hypothesis framed Schultz could quickly and ineffectively test it. There's tremendous power to this straightforward step. An orienting Harvard-featured study on the subject found that writing a formal hypothesis more than doubles the odds of idea testing, and effective idea testing is one of the strongest indicators of idea adoption and implementation.[59]

CASE IN PRACTICE: INTEL AI

Already the world's most valuable semiconductor company, the firm's acquisitions and R&D trajectory over a three-year span pointed to a new horizon strategy. Cognitive computing company Saffron Technology was purchased. Then Intel acquired computer vision firm

---

59   Washburn, N., & Hunsaker, B. T. (2011). Finding great ideas in emerging markets. Harvard Business Review.

Nervana Systems. Mobileye, an Israeli developer of autonomous driving systems, next joined the ranks in for $15.3 billion USD. Over the same period Intel was hard at work developing AI (artificial intelligence) and machine learning and vision capabilities, and related technologies, to support their growing IoT (internet of things) interests.

These are some of the actions the firm took to implement their new innovation focus. Before these actions, significant effort went into identifying the need and fleshing out the opportunity. What a group of effective Bridgers at Intel saw was a rapid trend acceleration toward AI, but an equally pronounced void of a single-source focused on providing developers with the ease of use, integration, and processing capacity needed to deliver cohesive responses from the center to the edge for their AI projects. User wanted this combination of power and ease of use, but it wasn't available in an integrated offering.

Here is that observation framed as a testable solution hypothesis:

> If our artificial intelligence approach provides every data scientist, developer and practitioner with access to the best platform and easiest starting point to solve the AI problem being tackled from the data center to the edge, then they'll prefer Intel as their partner of choice.

HYPOTHESIS TO REWARD:
HEALTHCARE AND AGRICULTURE

HEALTHCARE USE CASE

Few industries were more complex, with higher stakes, but also as big as healthcare. From diagnosis to care delivery, and the myriad administrative activities in between, every turn required precision. Coupled with rising costs, massive record keeping and reporting demands, increased procedure and equipment intricacy, and the growing global interest to democratize care the industry had no shortage of innovation need. Intel chose to begin in healthcare where the stakes were highest and with a target audience that felt these stakes most acutely with the following general hypothesis: If Intel-powered AI could repeatably improve diagnosis accuracy then patient outcomes will increase and attractive market rewards follow.

This hypothesis, accepted and implemented, provided the foundation for Intel's healthcare AI entry. Keen to support physicians and optimize the patient experience, Intel isolated several key intervention areas (and their related support functions) rife with diagnosis ambiguity. Results across a variety of healthcare organizations were compelling. Stanford Medical shortened image classification from 45 minutes to 1 minute. Mayo Clinic could better sift through big data to provide personalized care. Harvard Medical noted improved predictability in tumor response to chemotherapy. Physicians tasked to distinguish between like symptoms for a variety of heart ailments, ranging from mild to critical, saw diagnosis accuracy rates improve from 50% to nearly 90%.[60]

Emboldened by these successes and eager to initially complement rather than compete with healthcare providers, Intel developed early design principles for when AI should be used: 1) when a specialist can't be available 2) when inputs change in real-time 3) when solutions vary from patient to patient. When employed the results tended towards earlier diagnosis, with greater accuracy–while better utilizing existing resources. Intel General Manager at the time for the Saffron AI platform applied to heart disease described its power for improved patient outcomes,

> Before, for these types of diagnoses, you had to know what you were looking for; focus in on a few attributes–and in the process, human bias was introduced. The revolution here is being able to deliver higher accuracy based on all 10,000 attributes per heartbeat. It's a non-compromise scenario, which results in the best outcome.[61]

AGRICULTURE USE CASE

Equally pressing given the industry's vital-nature and scale was global food chains. Food security was a major concern; underproduction and waste typified practices in much of the world. Food

---

60 https://www.forbes.com/sites/patrickmoorhead/2018/03/21/intel-and-healthcare-partners-lean-into-ai-at-solve-event/#1d93b4de3d37. Retrieved 12 September 2019.

61 https://www.intel.com/content/www/us/en/healthcare-it/article/improved-diagnosis.html. Retrieved 07 September 2019.

contamination at the time alone cost the industry nearly $60 billion USD annually. Increasing global populations pressed the agriculture sector for better yields each year, and population growth models predicted a net increase of 2 billion by 2050–requiring production capacity to rise 50%.[62]

The combination of rising demand, relatively constrained natural resources, and agriculture's susceptibility to a variety of externalities (e.g. weather patterns, pests, drought) provided the dots for enterprising Intel Bridgers to connect the need for dramatically reshaped production input activities. Engaging with farmers in a variety of contexts revealed key opportunities for AI intervention. Early invasive pest detection, crop yield prediction, production-enhancing resource regulation, and harvesting techniques, all supported by AI-powered robotics, highlighted areas to grow more, for less, with increased reliability.

Success cases materialized quickly. Taylor Farms, one of the world's largest lettuce variety producers, reported increased precision from AI-powered automated harvesting. Sweden's BoMill engaged grain farmer to introduce, for the first time, reliable separation of good from bad grain at the point of the pick–resulting in a nearly 50% yield spike.

In North America alone growers lost nearly $5 billion USD annually to waste. AI-driven robotic herbicide application helped Taylor Farms to further the firm's mission to provide the highest-quality products while reducing reliance on chemicals, cutting herbicides use by a factor of nearly ten.

Intel believed these wins were just the beginning of what would be a radical shift in agriculture from primarily labor-intensive practices subject to a variety of externalities to technology-intensive and more predictable practices. The physical world of farming would increasingly converge with the digital world of technology–and both would benefit.

---

62   http://fortune.com/food-contamination/. Retrieved 22 September 2019.

Intel's end-to-end AI services strategy was designed to lead this shift — initially spurred by meaningful observation converted to succinct, testable hypothesis:

> If farmers have accessible data science and AI tools, they will be able to get the most from every acre.[63]

63   https://www.intel.com/content/www/us/en/big-data/article/
      agriculture-harvests-big-data.html. Retrieved 14 September
      2019.

Discovery section →

Part I: Respond

Respond to the questions below using the following rating scale:
A = Always.   B = Often.   C = Sometimes.   D = Rarely.   E = Never.

17. I take the additional step to turn observations into actionable opportunities?

18. I build out the intended persona for the opportunities I identify?

19. I take the time to turn my ideas into a testable hypothesis?

Part II: Describe

For the following questions, describe how you would most likely respond. To get the most from your efforts, **don't** describe what you *think you should do*, but rather *what you would most likely actually do* based on how you've responded to similar situations in the past.

You make an observation you think could be promising and you want to explore it further frame the potential opportunity. How would you do this?

How would you like your innovation approach to improve for having reviewed this chapter's insights? If you were asked to explain to others how to "Connect the Opportunity," what would you share?

Practice Activities Section

Choose an observation you'd like to consider for its opportunity potential. This can be from your current work or another aspect of life.

Step #1 — What are key elements in the Before, During, and After experience?

Describe the Observation. What is Liked, Disliked, and promotes Ambivalence about the current experience?

What is your initial idea to change the experience for good?

Step #2 — Frame the opportunity.

Where does the idea plot on the Opportunity Visualization Tool?

_____

_____

_____

_____

_____

_____

Does the idea reimagine inefficient monetization? Reconsider rent pockets?

_____

_____

_____

_____

_____

If not, from what does the idea derive its value?

_____

_____

_____

_____

_____

_____

The value of an insight is found in its doing. What are at least two concrete actions that can help you to more consistently "Connect the Opportunity?"

_____

_____

_____

_____

_____

_____

_____

What benefit(s) do you anticipate from doing these actions well?

_____

_____

_____

_____

_____

_____

_____

_____

_____

_____

_____

_____

_____

_____

_____

VALIDATION — INITIALLY TEST

While teaching a group of executives from the automotive and mobility industries in Latin America, one of the participants asked, "How do you know if an idea's any good?" A lively discussion ensued. Clearly, he wasn't the only one with this question. Controlling for operating conditions and implementation factors, the answer typically traces to understanding how well the idea was originally validated.

When successful and failed ideas are compared, the great ones typically have an initial line of evidence to predict their success that the failed ones lack.

Unsuspectingly, enterprises can be tempted to adopt ideas from people with overdeveloped confidence in their own intuition or to rely on focus groups—a few people chatting about something they know little about in an unnatural setting—to set innovation direction. Neither provides a repeatable process for answering, "is this a good idea?" before committing resources. Data transforms hunches into credible actions. The ability to quickly, inexpensively, and reliably validate ideas helps Bridgers to avoid engaging too deeply ideas that are unworthy of their attention or abandoning too quickly ideas that are.

Initial, effective validation for budding ideas is too uncommon — despite being straightforward and costing far less than backing a bad idea or rejecting a future game-changer. In the original *Harvard Business Review*-featured work on Bridgers, this author and colleagues found that less than half of the managers in the firms we studied who tried to find great ideas also initially validate their ideas. But all of the managers who validated their ideas also tried to win their adoption. Initial validation was key to ideas being shared, and over 30% of these ideas became successfully implemented game-changers.

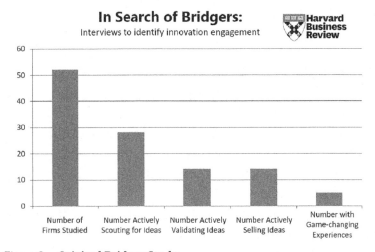

Figure 8 **Original Bridger Study**

DEEPENING THE CASE FOR VALIDATION

Consider this conceptual example for the role validation plays in initially vetting an idea's value and, done well, how naturally quality validation can flow from ideation to build credibility.

A company and industry have low market share for video and Internet services in a particularly attractive growth market segment (in this case the 30–45 age US Hispanic demographic) versus its general market. All levels of the company agree they want to maximize this growth opportunity. However, each time ideas to access this new growth segment are presented, they are run through the prevailing organizational structure and financial models. The results are typically a failed test or desk rejection.

A newcomer is hired to the company and goes about validation differently. She immediately hires a local Hispanic agency. She engages someone in the demographic with 5 years of company experience. This coalition set this executive on the path to truly understand the market, create some hypotheses of the challenges, and then test a few ideas.

They don't just conduct formal research through customer surveys and preset questioning techniques. They have lunch at some of the most popular Hispanic restaurants and invited people to openly talk. They speak with a range of constituents, among them potential target customers, community leaders, and elected officials. That level of immersion and authentic feedback provides foundational credibility that will come into play when presenting the business case to the company's Chief Marketing Officer (CMO).

Through these interactions and other efforts, the group finds that previous tactics were solving for the wrong problems. The firm's overall customer experience for the target Hispanic market demographic is the challenge. Specifically, the company's buying experience and promotional efforts do not resonate with the target market.

Using input from their interviews, observations, and research the team uncovers that the overall relationship and approach to this demographic needs to be reimagined. They create an initial list of ideas that they think will address this challenge. They run their ideas by trusted others who know the industry well — helping the group prioritize their ideas to properly test each. Checking these against previous ideas introduced to the company, the group realizes one of their most promising ideas was previously introduced to the company, but not adopted — largely for lack of initial evidence. The group determines to give the idea a better chance for success, and launches an envisioned scenario trial in one market.

The trial is successful.

With this initial validation experience to draw from, the group further sharpens the business case using their understanding of both the company and the target segment and comes up with ways to reduce the cost to launch the initiative and improve its returns.

This time the idea is embraced by the firm's CMO and other executives. Early returns show target segment performance exceeding goal, which deepens the firm's confidence to further invest in the initiative. Equally important, this group and broader company learn a valuable lesson about the power of initial validation they make part of their innovation approach going forward.

While generalized to underscore the overall concept, the principles in this example unfold globally thousands of times, each day.

Contrast the above with another example.

Lucas is a regional vice president in Eastern Europe. He works for a British company with operations throughout the globe. When we met, he expressed deep frustration with his home office. Executives there had repeatedly shut down his attempts to develop a modified product for the Eastern European market. Despite the negative response, Lucas kept trying.

He has clear opinions about why the product needed to change, why the modification would benefit his company, its distributors, and most importantly, its customers. Listening to him, he is certainly passionate about his idea. He believes the new offering would revolutionize not only his region, but other markets as well. Given his extensive experience in the industry and with the company, it is hard not to believe him. So why don't the company's executives?

Much of the explanation can be traced to validation. Asked to describe his idea, Lucas speaks impassionedly. He's also clearly willing to be persistent. But to the outside observer, he trades substance for fervor. His opinions are just that — his thoughts and feelings about what should be.

In his eagerness to evangelize his thinking, Lucas fails to bring credible evidence to the discussion beyond his own conviction. The idea never advances — leaving Lucas frustrated and the firm perhaps missing out on a valuable new insight.

WORTH ITS WEIGHT IN GOLD

Across varied demographics and geographies, gold is synonymous with value. This traces to its real and symbolic importance. From serving as currency itself or underpinning currency standards to marking marriage commitment through the exchange of gold rings, across history gold has been the element of choice. The process for uncovering gold, and its relative rarity, explain much of its perceived value.

From the early days of mining with hand pans to modern automated trommels, sifting has been critical to sluffing extraneous material to uncover pure gold. Focused effort has always been needed to determine whether and what caliber of gold exists — the essence of mining much to filter to what's of highest value.

It's little wonder that when it was time to describe the action of examining large databases to uncover key insights, the language chosen was *data mining*.

Gold and the value of validation have been related since at least the 200's BC when the famous Greek mathematician, physicist, and astronomer regarded as one of the all-time scientists, Archimedes had his now famous "Eureka!" moment. As the account goes, then King Hieron II of Syracuse in Sicily gave a goldsmith a bar of gold to make into a crown. After the goldsmith delivered the crown to the king, the king was suspicious of its purity. The king believed the goldsmith could have cheated him by mixing some of the pure gold with less valuable silver and keeping the difference for himself.[64][65]

The King's dilemma was he had no way to prove his suspicions. So, he tasked Archimedes with devising a way to determine the crown's purity. Adding to the task, Archimedes had to do so without damaging the crown.

---

64 Kuroki, H. (2016). How did Archimedes discover the law of buoyancy by experiment?. *Frontiers of Mechanical Engineering, 11*(1), 26-32.

65 Stein, S. (1999). Archimedes: *what did he do beside cry eureka?* (Vol. 11). MAA.

Archimedes told the king he would need a few days to consider how to validate the gold's purity. One day, his mind steeped in the challenge set before him by King Hieron, Archimedes decided to take a bath. Entering the water, he noticed that the water splashed out of his bath tub onto the floor the moment he stepped into it, and the more force he exerted, the water was displaced.

As if talking through the phenomenon with colleagues, Archimedes could have reasoned, "When I got into the tub, my body displaced the water relative to the weight provided. There must be a relationship between my volume and the volume of water that my body displaced—the heavier the weight of the force, the more water is displaced."

Perhaps the same phenomenon relates to the weight of the crown? Archimedes realized that object density could be validated by placing it in water.

Knowing gold was denser than silver, Archimedes placed a piece of pure gold into a container of water to measure the water displacement. He did the with a piece of silver of the same mass. Although both metals had the same mass, the silver had a larger volume; so, it displaced more water than did the gold. Archimedes realized that if a certain amount of silver had been substituted for the same amount of gold, the crown would occupy a larger space compared to an identical amount of pure gold. This would mean that if the goldsmith had made a crown of pure gold, then the volume displaced should be the same as that of a bar of pure gold of the same mass.

Carrying the simple experiment forward, with limited resources Archimedes had quickly and successfully demonstrated that the goldsmith had indeed mixed silver into the crown's fabrication.[66][67][68]

---

66 Dijksterhuis, E. J. (2014). Archimedes. Princeton University Press.

67 Price, H. (1997). *Time's arrow & Archimedes' point: new directions for the physics of time.* Oxford University Press, USA.

68 Thompson, F. (2008). Archimedes and the golden crown. *Physics Education, 43*(4), 396.

From Archimedes' interactions with King Hieron to the most digitally advanced proposals of the present day, no idea, regardless of how well conceived, is ready for wholesale adoption before going through initial validation. Equally important, poor ideas presented beautifully can unmasked for what they really are through effective validation.

Initial validation is the pivotal gate for assessing idea quality.

Techniques to successfully validate, quickly and with limited time and resources, are outlined in the next chapters.

Figure 9   **Sifting for Gold**

Discovery section →

Part I: Respond

Respond to the questions below using the following rating scale:
A = Always.   B = Often.   C = Sometimes.   D = Rarely.   E = Never.

20. I initially validate my ideas before trying to sell them?

21. When I've sufficiently considered an idea, I skip initial validation to save time?

22. I view initial validation as resource — dependent; when I have the resources I do it?

Part II: Describe

For the following questions, describe how you would most likely respond. To get the most from your efforts, **don't** describe what you *think you should do*, but rather *what you would most likely actually do* based on how you've responded to similar situations in the past.

You believe you have a promising idea. What is your next action and why?

_____

_____

_____

_____

_____

_____

_____

_____

_____

_____

_____

_____

Suggested responses to Part I: A, D, D

How would you like your innovation approach to improve for having reviewed this chapter's insights? If you were asked to explain to others the importance of initial "Validation: Refining," what would you share?

Practice Activities Section

Choose an idea you believe has promise and complete the following sections with this idea in mind.

Step #1 — How does the idea differ from the current norm?

Describe in what ways the idea differs from the current norm.

_____

_____

_____

_____

_____

_____

_____

How did you think this may influence the way those who have a vested interest in the current norm perceive the idea?

_____

_____

_____

_____

_____

_____

_____

_____

_____

_____

_____

_____

DISCOVERY SECTION

Step #2 — Envision how initial validation can help you to overcome these barriers.

How would evidence help you to reduce skepticism about the idea?

What forms of evidence could be most beneficial?

The value of an insight is found in its doing. What are at least two concrete actions that can help you to more consistently engaging in "Validation?"

What benefit(s) do you anticipate from doing these actions well?

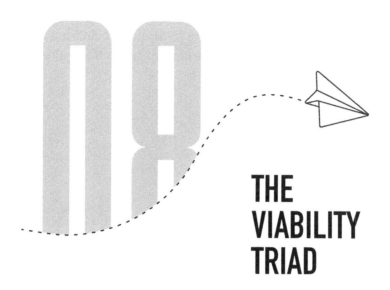

THE
VIABILITY
TRIAD

The heavy weight of choosing among options is summed up in this quote by Winston Churchill, found in Richard Langworth's *Churchill by Himself*: "A (wo)man must answer 'aye' or 'no' to the great questions, and by that decision he must be bound." Real and opportunity costs loom largely when choosing where to commit additional resources.

While Churchill dealt with wartime crises, leaders on other fronts face increased competition, complex stakeholder relationships, operating ambiguity, and rising costs amid budget constraints. But they still are aided by answering "aye" or "no" to a series of great questions. And, in doing so, they often must overcome a great degree of uncertainty.

During a pointed conversation with a CEO of a large multinational firm, he expressed that one of his job's biggest challenges is to know when his decisions are on the right track—before it's too late. No decision is greater than choosing which ideas to pursue.

While it's impossible to predict with certainty the outcome of any innovation, effective validation helps decision makers to understand the likelihood of success before they overcommit resources. The Viability Triad focuses validation outputs on three key questions that help evaluate the potential for an idea's success.[69] Like the quality of a home's foundation, everything else rests on getting these elements right.

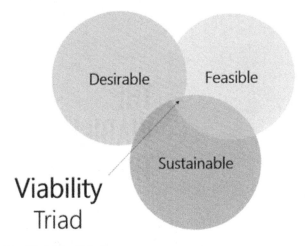

Desirable

Feasible

Sustainable

Viability
Triad

Figure 10   **Viability Triad**

CONSIDERING DESIRABILITY

The first great question is: Is it valuable? That is, is the idea anchored to relevant behavioral trends? Will a lot of people want it? If not, will a smaller segment pay a premium for it?

A perfect example of misdiagnosing desirability is provided by Apple's release of the Newton, the product for which the phrase "personal digital assistant" was coined. When the Newton was launched in the mid-1990s, Apple expected it to make handheld computing ubiquitous. By 1998, the product had been canceled. Apple—which has been uncommonly successful in understanding and shaping consumer preferences—miscalculated behavioral trends. The Newton was too far ahead of the adoption curve, and consumers failed to see why they needed an expensive toy that mimicked the function of a paper notepad.

69   Hunsaker, B. T., & Thomas, D. E. (2017). The Viability Triad: Desirability, Feasibility, and Sustainability as the New Strategic Decision Imperative. *Journal of Management, 5*(2), 1-4.

Fast forward to the development of the iPhone and the iPad. While the iPad was developed first, Apple chose to lead with the iPhone in 2007. Why? Company leaders had a better understanding of behavioral trends at the time.

By the time the iPhone was introduced cell phones were already common. Apple's revolutionary additions were the iPhone's sleek touchscreen interface and the robust vertical integration. Apple capitalized on the existing behavioral trend of cell phone adoption, and then radically transformed the caliber of that experience. The firm had found the ideal balance for introducing value-centered innovation into a ready adoption curve.

A similar scenario can be seen in higher education. When administrators decide to support programs that are not grounded in relevant behavioral trends, they run the risk of diluting resources, unnecessarily increasing complexity, and disconnecting their programs from reality. They can make these decisions passively, by simply allowing outdated content models or teaching modalities to continue. Or they can make these decisions actively, by embracing programs even when it's not clear that they will have good outcomes. In both cases, they have failed to acknowledge that these programs are not desirable.

IS IT VALUABLE? SUPPORT QUESTIONS:

- Is it anchored to relevant behavioral trends?
- Will a lot of people want it, often?
- If not, will a smaller segment pay a lot and depend on it?

CONSIDERING FEASIBILITY

There is an important difference between envisioning new horizons and committing resources to unfounded pursuits. Therefore, the second great question is: Can it be done? Is the experience possible, both technically and politically? Can the necessary resources be accessed? Can the idea be operationalized in the allotted timeframe? If the answers are no, leaders should be concerned.

The University of California's all-digital online campus provides a compelling feasibility warning. During a short burst window of exuberance, the already cash-strapped university system poured nearly US$10 million into an initiative that returned only a fraction of its investment. At the base level, the MOOC system that university leaders envisioned was possible, but it depended on providing an educational experience that would attract both matriculated students and students from outside the UC system.

It largely failed to meet experience demands relative to its cost, and student enrollment from outside UC never materialized. The MOOC approach burdened resources that were already in short supply, relied on demand that didn't exist, and couldn't succeed within the estimated timeframe. The university system eventually swallowed the cost within its budget.

Ideally, feasible projects unfold in progressive stages: opportunity, validation, development, optimization, scale. Projects that aren't feasible tend to follow a more regressive and emotionally-charged pattern: euphoria, concern, panic, disillusionment, and blame. Whenever leaders are faced with a big decision, they first should determine feasibility by iterating and validating an opportunity before committing larger resources that may be better leveraged elsewhere.

CAN IT BE DONE? SUPPORT QUESTIONS:

- Is it technically possible?
- Is it politically possible?
- Can the needed resources be accessed?
- Can the organization operationalize the idea in the allotted timeframe?

CONSIDERING SUSTAINABILITY

It's not enough for an idea to be superficially attractive; it also must have staying power. Therefore, the third great question is:

Should it be done? Will it generate the intended returns, now and later? Is it repeatable, resilient, and difficult to imitate? Does it rely on economic, intellectual, and environmental resources that are renewable or in abundant supply?

A commitment to environmental stewardship is only one component of long-term sustainability, but it's an important one. Organizations like Unilever, Toyota, DuPont, GE, Patagonia, Henkel, IKEA, and P&G have successfully positioned environmental sustainability as a strategic imperative.

But other forms of sustainability also have become crucial to businesses today, largely because of two shifts in mindset. First, firms that have flipped their focus from driving down costs to pursuing greater efficiency have improved their returns, developed more durable processes, and created stronger barriers to competition, while utilizing fewer resources. Second, these organizations have set a tone in their value chains that ripples into the operations of their partners and suppliers. A more nimble, responsive value chain is better able to leverage resources, reduce waste, and scale operations.

Those who encounter fierce competition sometimes tempted to trade long-term sustainability for short-term gains. A laser focus on sustainability is more likely to create abundant returns over time.

SHOULD IT BE DONE? SUPPORT QUESTIONS:

- Will it generate the intended returns, now and later?
- Is it efficient, internally consistent, & resource responsive?
- Is it repeatable and resilient?
- Is it difficult for others to imitate?

CLARITY AMIDST COMPLEXITY

An abbreviated definition for "viable" is "likely to succeed." In dynamic operating environments, there's too much at stake to make decisions with anything less than success in mind. Too often, however, the complexity of a decision shifts the focus away from the most important things that clarify otherwise challenging determinations. As a result, initiatives fail.

Though Churchill didn't outline which questions to ask, he paved the way by qualifying that a few great questions should take precedence above others for their ability to cut through the noise and focus on what matters most. Just as simplistic approaches stand in the way of great decisions by considering too little, so does needless complexity. Before proceeding with any project, answers to the three great questions of the viability triad should be considered: Is it valuable? Can it be done? Should it be done?

Embedding these great questions into the validation process trains your line of sight on what is most relevant to the success of any decision. And when you can confidently answer "aye" to the great questions, you're likely to produce outcomes to which you will gladly be bound

The Viability Triad provides the analytical framework to put ideas initially to the test. Think of this as a vehicle's engine — providing guided action capacity to the validation process. Just an energy source is needed to power the vehicle forward, the techniques outlined in the next chapter provide the input data support to bring the Viability Triad's guiding questions to life: Is it valuable? Can it be done? Should it be done?

Discovery section →

Part I: Respond

Respond to the questions below using the following rating scale:
A = Always.   B = Often.   C = Sometimes.   D = Rarely.   E = Never.

23. I consider an idea's desirability
    before promoting it?

24. I consider an idea's feasibility
    before promoting it?

25. I consider an idea's sustainability
    before promoting it?

Part II: Describe

For the following questions, describe how you would most likely respond. To get the most from your efforts, **don't** describe what you *think you should do*, but rather *what you would most likely actually do* based on how you've responded to similar situations in the past.

You've scouted a new idea and seek an initial understanding of its viability to support your validation efforts. How do you go about this?

Suggested responses to Part I: A, A, A

125

How would you like your innovation approach to improve for having reviewed this chapter's insights? If you were asked to explain to others the benefits of the "Viability Triad," what would you share?

Practice Activities Section

Choose an idea you believe has promise and complete the following sections with this idea in mind.

Step #1 — How does the idea initially perform on the Viability Triad questions?

DESIRABLE Is it valued? What support do you have for your response?

_____

_____

_____

_____

_____

FEASIBLE Can it be done? What support do you have for your response?

_____

_____

_____

_____

_____

_____

SUSTAINABLE Should it be done? What support do you have for your response?

_____

_____

_____

_____

_____

_____

_____

Step #2 — Envision how the Viability Triad can help to frame your validation efforts.

Why does the order you engage the Viability Triad's questions matter?

_____

_____

_____

_____

_____

_____

_____

_____

_____

How do the Viability Triad's questions provide an analytical framework for you to engage validation — and inform related decisions?

_____

_____

_____

_____

_____

_____

_____

_____

_____

_____

_____

_____

The value of an insight is found in its doing. What are at least two concrete actions that can help you to more consistently utilize the "Viability Triad?"

What benefit(s) do you anticipate from doing these actions well?

VALIDATION STRATEGIES

I f the Viability Triad frames great questions to increase odds for supporting the right innovations, the validation strategies in this chapter operationalize these questions and provide the information to answer the great questions: Is it valuable? Can it be done? Should it be done?

Data transforms hunches into credible opportunities. Before developing a full prototype or even minimum viable product you can use certain techniques to understand whether it is worthwhile to commit further resources to those efforts. The ability to inexpensively, quickly, and reliably validate ideas builds objective support for further development.

Effective Bridgers are skilled in three validation methods.

SIMPLE EXPERIMENTATION

The experience of a once fledgling franchisee in a high-profile quick casual restaurant chain provides key insights into how simple experimentation can test an idea's viability. An early franchisee in Latin America, his excitement quickly turned to frustration as the sales he expected did not materialize. Fearful of losing his business, he carefully began to study the behaviors of customers.

He noted that while customers liked the brand's chicken, they saw little value in the rest of the menu. He thought that inserting local side dishes to the menu could improve his business, so he contacted headquarters and requested permission to adapt the local menu. His request was denied.

At the time, this company was committed to a strategy that tried to minimize variation in its international operations. While there were sound reasons for this approach (e.g. economies of scale and operational simplicity), none of these were satisfying to this franchisee who risked losing the large investment he had made in multiple restaurant locations. What he did next not only transformed his existing business, but he would go on to become a larger franchisee in the brand's system and help the firm to realize the power of strategic localization, an approach the company has used to great international success.

To A/B testing (shorthand for a controlled simple experiment) his hypothesis, he set aside a portion of one of his locations for an inexpensive experiment (the other locations were untouched to serve as a control). Using a simple sign, he prompted customers that they could substitute side dishes on the menu for local rice and beans. The rice and beans combination sold out.

Persuaded that he had a good idea he expanded his test to a location on the other side of town. Sales climbed in both locations as word spread of the combination of the brand's signature chicken with localized side dishes. The next conversation with headquarters went much differently. With minimal expense, this franchisee had succeeded in replacing the skepticism that first greeted his idea with enthusiasm for a new growth strategy. A simple experiment helped headquarters to appreciate what he did.

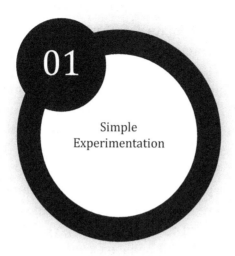

Simple
Experimentation

Hunches alone can't determine an idea's potential. **Simple Experimentation** quickly and inexpensively tests for viability by bringing the essence of an idea to life to understand how it may work in practice.

ENVISIONED SCENARIOS

When simple experimentation is not possible envisioned scenarios are a valuable proxy. Envisioned scenarios elaborate for target consumers an alternate reality (the new idea) to their current experience, and ask them to place themselves in that new reality and provide feedback. This is done in their natural setting (at the point of sale, for example) to elicit grounded input.

Facing increased competition and with an eye to the company's aggressive growth arc, a 3M brand manager needed to invigorate sales for a specialty product targeting the professional electrician market. The manager hypothesized that if electricians better understood the longevity and safety benefits of the product, they'd be more likely to pay a premium for it. Facing stiff competition from inferior but less expensive alternatives, the company risked losing market share if they didn't take a new approach.

Durability over time is difficult to validate through experimentation when immediate data is needed. Instead, this manager utilized an envisioned scenario to proximate how electricians would value the longevity and safety theme. A team was sent to various job sites representative of the target market (professional electricians) where they asked, "If you had access to a product just as easy to apply but lasted twice as long and nearly eliminated fire risk would you pay a few more dollars to use it in your projects?"

Over 90% responded affirmatively. The team also noted that the responses were largely immediate and assertive (suggesting stronger commitment to the feedback given). While not a guarantee that customers will behave exactly the way they describe, the envisioned scenario provides targeted input from more natural settings — improving data quality. This supplied the brand manager needed support to anchor the product message to the longevity and safety theme.

Envisioned scenarios also help people to break from previously help positions to consider the alternative by introducing them to new information — a critical element to effective validation.

This is just what happened when the Brookings Institution found attitudes were largely based on perceptions of how much government spends on foreign aid and how that aid is spent.

Public opinion polls find the majority of U.S. citizens believe the U.S. spends around 20% of its annual budget on foreign aid. With this perception in mind, over half of Americans believe the government spends too much on foreign aid.

Foreign aid actually averages just 1% of the federal budget — significantly less than many other budget items.

Brookings then employed the envisioned scenario technique to gauge public opinion based on grounded data rather than misguided perception.

"Asked to 'imagine that you found out that the U.S. spends 1% of the federal budget on foreign aid,' the number saying the U.S. spends too much drops to 26%."[70]

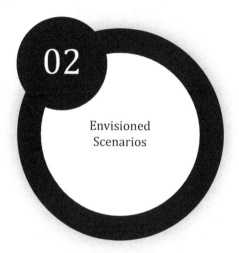

Envisioned
Scenarios

The **Envisioned Scenario Survey** technique effectively describes for target consumers the solution "as if" it exists and captures their likelihood to adopt based on this potential. This provides Bridgers with important feedback and insights related to how people will likely respond to a given idea — before it's actually built.

---

70   https://fas.org/sgp/crs/row/R40213.pdf. Retrieved February 17, 2020.

Hypothesis	Validate Using Envisioned Scenario	Responses
A testable proposed explanation for a phenomenon	If (insert alternative reality), then (insert intended outcome)	Input as a numeric value (over 90% threshold desired) RESPONSE STRENGTH INDICATORS Weak – Delayed &passive Immediate and passive Delayed and assertive Strong – Immediate & assertive
EXAMPLE *Electricians will pay a premium if they understand the product's significant longevity and safety benefits.*	EXAMPLE *If you had access to a product just as easy to use but lasted twice as long and nearly eliminated fire risk over that time would you pay a few more dollars to use it in your projects?*	EXAMPLE *> 90% immediate and assertive* **(Strongest)**

Figure 11   **Envisioned Scenario Wireframe**

COMMONALITY BENCHMARKING

When leadership for an international division of Johnson & Johnson wanted to validate their idea for the country's next growth areas(s) they turned to commonality benchmarking. To do so they isolated success indicators in existing markets, benchmarked these variables to a range of potential new growth markets, and filtered commonalities to identify relevant patterns. In several cases what emerged from the validation effort supported their ideas for where to make their next move. The findings also prevented them from misallocating resources to other areas they had initially identified.

Commonality benchmarking brings objectivity to selecting among idea options. For example, the Johnson & Johnson team received input from their sales staff and their distributor network about areas that would offer the best growth potential. The country manager also had his own ideas about the company's next move. Both were hunches until put through the validation process.

The value of commonality benchmarking is it allows managers to use a known standard to distinguish indicative patterns from anomalies. It is most useful when a clear picture for success indicators can be established (e.g. demographic indicators, channel vitality indicators, promotion response indicators, among others) and data for comparison cases are available. In the Johnson & Johnson illustration this approach was used within the firm's own operational footprint, but it can also be used across organizations or industries. For example, comparing predicted success factors of a new idea to the known success indicators of relevant existing firms and isolating commonalities can provide insight into the likelihood for the desired outcome. Rather than mimicry (superficial resemblance), this technique intends to increase predictability for original ideas. Ideally, this approach is used in combination with simple experimentation or envisioned scenarios to provide multiple layers of validation.

Ideas often share common elements with proven examples. **Commonality benchmarking** compares and contrasts the idea to relevant best practices.

SIZE THE PRIZE

Understanding scalability and intended impact, 'sizing of the prize,' are important considerations for whether to pursue an innovation. To complement the intelligence from initial validation, unpacking an innovation's potential reach further informs unpacks its desirability. Two tools can help.

Knowing the potential market size distinguishes a nice idea from a sweepingly valuable innovation. The equation in Exhibit 12 can be used to produce a quantitative output for the economic opportunity.

$$Sz = TC * F * P \qquad ROI = \frac{Sz - Cost}{Cost}$$

Sz= Market size in appropriate currency
TC= (Establish likely client persona) Total number of predicted actual clients
F= Frequencyof annual purchase(s) 1-5
P= Price point

Exhibit 12   **Size the Prize Market Equation**

In some cases, sizing the prize is better expressed by impact rather than sales. For example, an innovation to radically optimize an internal organizational process is better expressed as impact magnitude than market opportunity. In these instances, the following can be substituted: M = EX*F*P

M= Magnitude (example: a sales department process)
EX= Predicted number of process exchanges influenced
F= Frequency of influenced annual exchange(s)
P= Estimated value of exchanges (revenue generating or cost saving)

Understanding an innovation's potential for scale also helps to size the prize. The Scale Score (SC) tool gives a numeric value for the idea's scalability. The higher the total SC output, the greater the innovation's potential for scale.

Not all innovation is (or should be) built to scale. The SC tool helps Bridgers to avoid asking of an innovation something it's not built to provide — or setting expectations with others likely to go unmet.

Exhibit 13   **Scalability Score Card (SC)**

Skill or Practice	Score	Operating Cost Per Unit	Score	Adaptation	Score	Automation	Score	Trend	Score	Barriers to Mass Adoption	Score
Based on a skill or practice that is difficult to replicate consistently		Operating cost per unit rises with growth		Requires complete customization		Cannot be automated		Declining market		Very high	
Based on a skill or practice that can only marginally be replicated		Operating cost per unit stays the same with growth		Requires significant customization		Automation potential is limited		Stagnant market		High	
Based on a skill or practice that can moderately be replicated		Operating cost per unit marginally declines with growth		Requires partial customization		Can be partially automated		Low growth market		Moderate	
Based on a skill or practice that can largely be replicated		Operating cost per unit moderately declines with growth		Requires limited customization		Can be largely automated		Growth market		Low	
Based on a skill or practice that can be readily and consistently replicated		Operating cost per unit significantly declines with growth		Responsively standardized		Can be easily and fully automated		High growth market		Very low	

(low scalability = 1 med-low scalability = 2 medium scalability=3 med-high scalability =4 high scalability = 5)

139

ITERATION & INITIAL INDICATORS

Few innovations are perfect from the onset. Initial validation highlights their promise and continuous refinement makes them audience-ready.

Effective iteration nudges the worthy innovation, ideally quickly, through three important gates. The first represents and idea's early stage. An observation or connection is made, but few questions have been asked or data collected about the idea. It is superficially intriguing, but more is needed to confidently commit resources.

As more information is gathered, intricacy rises — multiple challenges, alternatives and variations surface. But the idea's fit-to-purpose isn't clear. Like gathering thousands of data points without turning them into useful insights, overwhelmingly, ideas left in this state fail to attract support. Another gate must be passed.

Validation and iteration work together. As the former brings viability information to light, the latter puts this information to work to refine the innovation — adding needed questions and then chipping away superfluous elements and complexity to reach precision. Tracking this progression is aided by the Iteration Progress Tool in Exhibit 15.

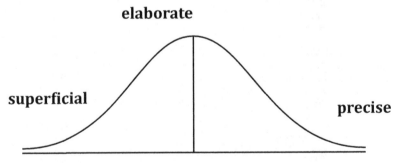

Exhibit 14   **Refinement Progression**

Iteration Progress Indicator

Test

Step 1: Hypothesis
We believe that...

Step 2: Test
To Verify that, we will...

Step 3: Metric
And measure...

Step 4: Criteria
We are right if...

Learning

Step 1: Hypothesis
We believed that....

Step 2: Observation
We noticed...

Step 3: Learning & Insights
From that we learned that...

Step 4: Decisions & Actions
Therefor we will...

Exhibit 15 **Tracking Progress**

Discovery section →

Part I: Respond

Respond to the questions below using the following rating scale:
A = Always.   B = Often.   C = Sometimes.   D = Rarely.   E = Never.

26. I look for ways to use simple experimentation to validate ideas? ☐

27 When simple experimentation isn't feasible, I conduct envisioned scenarios? ☐

28. I use commonality benchmarking to support my other validation efforts? ☐

Part II: Describe

For the following questions, describe how you would most likely respond. To get the most from your efforts, **don't** describe what you *think you should do*, but rather *what you would most likely actually do* based on how you've responded to similar situations in the past.

You've scouted a new idea and need to validate it. How will you do this?

_____

_____

_____

_____

_____

_____

_____

_____

_____

_____

_____

_____

Suggested responses to Part I: D, A, A

How would you like your innovation approach to improve for having reviewed this chapter's insights? If you were asked to explain to others how to put into practice "Validation Strategies," what would you share?

Practice Activities Section

Choose an idea you consider to be promising, but that has not yet been physically tested.

Step #1 — How could you validate the idea using each technique below?

SIMPLE EXPERIMENT

_____

_____

_____

_____

ENVISIONED SCENARIO

_____

_____

_____

_____

_____

COMMONALITY BENCHMARING

_____

_____

_____

_____

_____

_____

DISCOVERY SECTION

Step #2 — In this case, which method would you pursue further? Why?

The value of an insight is found in its doing. What are at least two concrete actions that can help you to more consistently use "Validation Strategies?"

DISCOVERY SECTION

What benefit(s) do you anticipate from doing these actions well?

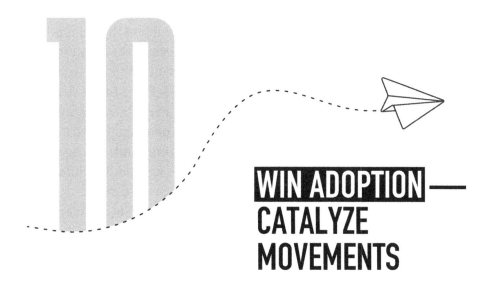

WIN ADOPTION — CATALYZE MOVEMENTS

Noted sociologist and professor Cristian Smith wrote of the tension between new ideas and existing norms, "One of the privileges of dominance is to not have to learn and think as hard as one should. Peripheral voices, by comparison, have got to think very hard about their claims."[71]

No idea is consequential until others embrace it. Because the inclination of many is to deflect ideas that don't match prevailing norms, Bridgers must be intentional about winning adoption for their ideas and catalyzing related movements.[72][73][74]

Broadly understanding social movements — both successful and unsuccessful — can help.

Nelson Mandela (who would go on to be South Africa's first democratically elected president) knew that alone he could have

71 https://www.youtube.com/watch?v=QK_G97It_JA. Retrieved December 16, 2019.

72 Della Porta, D., & Diani, M. (2020). Social movements: *An introduction.* John Wiley & Sons.

73 Gould, R. V. (1991). Multiple networks and mobilization in the Paris Commune, 1871. *American Sociological Review,* 716-729.

74 Snow, D. A., Zurcher Jr, L. A., & Ekland-Olson, S. (1980). Social networks and social movements: A microstructural approach to differential recruitment. *American sociological review,* 787-801.

little effect on South African apartheid. Something of that magnitude would require a social movement well beyond the influence of a single person. But how could such a movement take shape?

Mandela's words from his *Speech on the Dock* are instructive, "I have fought against white domination, and I have fought against black domination. I have cherished the ideal of a democratic and free society in which all persons live together in harmony and with equal opportunities. It is an ideal which I hope to live for and to achieve. But if needs be, it is an ideal for which I am prepared to die."[75]

Four keys to movement building are found in this short excerpt from Mandel's speech: 1) idea-anchored, 2) process-oriented, 3) relational, and 4) iterative.

While Mandela delivered his speech to a large audience, his aim was for it to reach individuals in personalized ways rather than wash over the masses. He knew that road adoption depended first on targeted adoption. When stating "all persons live together in harmony and with equal opportunities," Mandela's words translated could have easily read "each person."

In Mandela's wisdom, despite being the spokesperson for the budding movement, he focused on the concept (the idea for innovators) — clearly articulated — and not his role as spokesperson. This allowed others to see themselves in the idea and, like the snowball effect, to envision their own contribution and benefit. Authority accrued to Mandela and legitimacy to the movement as he strategically engaged others and allowed them to make the idea their own.

Though less romantic than often dramatically depicted, this speech was more the result of concerted effort than a spontaneous uprising. Mandela and others who embraced the movement acted purposefully, in an organized manner, and with all deliberate speed to build followership — similar to the way increasing concentric circles extend from a common core.

---

75 Mandela, N. (1990). *Nelson Mandela: The Struggle is My Life: His Speeches and Writings Brought Together with Historical Documents and Accounts of Mandela in Prison by Fellow-prisoners.* Popular Prakashan.

Some see irony in Mandela's decry of black domination during a speech clearly focused on ending white minority inspired apartheid. Others see brilliance. Mandela was simultaneously strength-signaling and coalition-building; for the movement to succeed it could not be 'us against them' but rather would build from the inclusive, shared benefit of a great new idea.

Mandela's closing lines highlight the iterative nature of movement building. Not all at once nor initially perfect, but nonetheless worthy of hearty backing, the validated ideal is consistently refined — improved upon as it is put into motion.

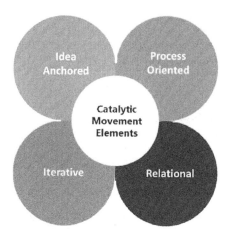

Figure 16   **Catalytic Movement General Elements**

Contrast this with the failed resistance efforts of young activists in Lithuania during World War II. The United Partisans Organization (*Fareinikte Partizaner Organizatsie*, or FPO) was a leftist youth upstart intent to lead the Vilna ghetto community to resist the Nazis — becoming among the first recorded attempts at Jewish resistance in Nazi-occupied Eastern Europe.[76][77]

---

76   Einwohner, Rachel L. 2007. "Leadership, Authority, and Collective Action: Jewish Resistance in the Ghettos of Warsaw and Vilna." *American Behavioral Scientist* 50(10): 1306-26.

77   Gamson, William A. 1990. The Strategy of Social Protest (2nd ed). Belmont, CA: Wadsworth Publishing.

Recruitment efforts included mass communication via activist networks seeking like-minded adherents. Yet, despite expending significant energy for the cause the FPO was not able to mobilize masses in the Vilna Ghetto. Purdue scholar Rachel Einwhoner provides telling insights for the failure (despite other successful ghetto uprisings, including the well-documented Warsaw experience):

> Despite their efforts, however, the FPO was not able to mobilize the masses in the Vilna Ghetto. In the summer of 1943, the Gestapo became aware of the identity of Itzhak Witenberg, one of the leaders of the FPO, and threatened to destroy the Ghetto unless Witenberg was turned over to them. The Ghetto community clamored for Witenberg, who had gone into hiding, to turn himself in; he eventually did so, and died in Nazi custody the next day. Given the community's lack of support for Witenberg, the rest of the FPO members reluctantly decided to abandon their plans for armed struggle in the ghetto and chose instead to escape to nearby forests to fight along with Soviet partisan units. Some FPO members did stage a brief battle when German soldiers entered the ghetto on September 1, 1943, but the Ghetto masses did not join them. The surviving FPO members then left for the forests and the Ghetto was liquidated on September 23, 1943.

> Part of the reason why the FPO was not able to mobilize the masses was that it lacked authority in the ghetto; rather than supporting the FPO, the ghetto masses followed the Nazi-appointed leader Jacob Gens, who encouraged ghetto residents not to resist but instead to work in ghetto factories supplying the German war effort and thereby demonstrate their utility to the Nazis.

> But what happened after the FPO's failed mobilization attempt is just as important as why it failed. The failure in the ghetto gave the FPO the opportunity to continue their resistance efforts elsewhere. In fact, once they fled the ghetto, some former FPO members became well known partisans who managed not only to survive the difficult conditions in the forests but also to carry out numerous acts of sabotage against German forces and even to join the Red Army in liberating Vilna in 1944.

> Even the most noble idea can miss the mark without the right adoption approach; the ability to win adoption for ideas is as important as the idea itself. In many ways, the world's great developments depend on this competency. [78]

Think of Bill Gates' ability to secure Microsoft's early adoption from IBM — and in the process catalyze the personal computer revolution largely running Microsoft software. This also helps to explain how at least fifteen other search engines existed when Google launched, but it was Google that won broad innovation adoption. Or, how Facebook soared when Myspace stalled.[79] [80]

Behind every significant innovation is someone who was able to motivate others to embrace the idea and wisely build on that nucleus.

Tracing founder stories globally yields many and rich tales of small teams of entrepreneurs catalyzing broad adoption for their innovations. Phil Knight of Nike, Adaora Mbelu-Dania of A2 Creative, Divyank Turakhia of media.net, Richard Branson of Virgin, Tina Sharkey of Brandless, and J. Willard Marriott of Marriott International, to name a few, all share something in common — they embraced key social science principles to get their ideas implemented.

But for every successful adoption there are thousands of otherwise strong ideas tossed into garbage bins around the world — every day — because their authors couldn't get others to embrace them.

Building on decades of leading social science research and innovation diffusion practice, winning adoption for gamechanger ideas funnels into two primary channels: messengers and messages.

The next two chapters focus on bringing these themes to life.

---

78   Einwohner, Rachel L. 2007. "Leadership, Authority, and Collective Action: Jewish Resistance in the Ghettos of Warsaw and Vilna." *American Behavioral Scientist* 50(10): 1306-26.

79   Robards, B. (2012). Leaving MySpace, joining Facebook:'Growing up'on social network sites. *Continuum, 26*(3), 385-398.

80   Mustaffa, N., Ibrahim, F., Mahmud, W. A. W., Ahmad, F., Kee, C. P., & Mahbob, M. H. (2011). Diffusion of innovations: The adoption of Facebook among youth in Malaysia. *The Public Sector Innovation Journal,* 16(3), 1-15.

Discovery section →

Part I: Respond

Respond to the questions below using the following rating scale:
A = Always.   B = Often.   C = Sometimes.   D = Rarely.   E = Never.

29. The first person I'm likely to share an idea with in someone I think will agree with it?

30. I consider how movements form before trying to sell my ideas?

31. I'm quick to change how I approach getting my ideas across when shown a better way?

Part II: Describe

For the following questions, describe how you would most likely respond. To get the most from your efforts, **don't** describe what you *think you should do*, but rather *what you would most likely actually do* based on how you've responded to similar situations in the past.

You believe one of your ideas is promising. But it will change how others around you must operate, so you suspect it will be met with resistance. What do you do next?

_____

_____

_____

_____

_____

_____

_____

_____

_____

_____

Suggested responses to Part I: D, B, B

How would you like your innovation approach to improve for having reviewed this chapter's insights? If you were asked to explain to others key takeaways from "Win Adoption — Catalyze Movement," what would you share?

Practice Activities Section

Choose an idea you consider to be promising. Outline how the four keys to building movements could be helpful as you seek to win its adoption.

Step #1 — What can you apply to research on building movements to support winning adoption for your idea?

IDEA-ANCHORED

_____

_____

_____

_____

PROCESS-ORIENTED

_____

_____

_____

_____

RELATIONAL

_____

_____

_____

_____

ITERATIVE

_____

_____

_____

_____

DISCOVERY SECTION

Step #2 — What can you apply from failed movements to this scenario?

The value of an insight is found in its doing. What are at least two concrete actions you can employ from "Win Adoption — Catalyze Movement?"

What benefit(s) do you anticipate from doing these actions well?

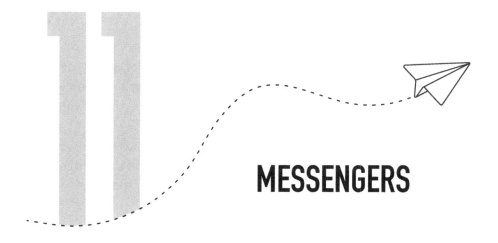

MESSENGERS

Why is this called a chair? The question came with little warning during a family gathering on a warm summer's day. The ten-year-old girl asking the question seemed genuinely curious — ready to hear her father's reply. Her father was less ready to answer.

"Because the person who invented it wanted to call it by that name."

The young girl pressed for more, not realizing the wisdom in her next question.

"So, we call it a chair because others followed the inventor?" Grateful her question also provided the answer, her father followed,

"Exactly. When a lot of people agree on something that's where it gets its meaning."

Little could have warned this dad that he would field that question on that day. In this simple exchange, he and his daughter arrived at an understanding underpinned by decades of leading social science research about the adoption of innovation. Together, they came to appreciate that new concepts are arbitrary until others assign them value. Legitimacy for new ideas comes from others embracing them. It's in their shared meaning and adoption that promising ideas can transform into breakthrough innovations.

BUILD A CASE

Potentially valuable ideas go unnoticed daily because the idea's sponsor couldn't get others to accept them. Innovation, by definition, changes or otherwise alters an existing norm. Recognizing that it's always easier to do nothing than something new, skilled Bridgers intentionally build idea legitimacy.

Two approaches are particularly useful: utilizing advocates and sharpening message quality. This chapter focuses on messengers and the power of advocacy.

POWER OF ADVOCATES

Complacency and risk aversion are powerful impediments to needed change. Overcoming the propensity to deflect ideas that fall outside existing norms is aided by skillfully engaging advocates.

Adoption of new ideas is not viewed equally by all. Some people are willing to stand out and will invest the time to understand an idea's merit. Among this group are a smaller segment whom others consider influential. The majority of people take their cues from watching to see if an initial crowd will form around an idea before jumping in. Their perception of an idea's merit is tied to influential crowd affiliation. In any group, this tends to describe the greater percentage of people.[81][82][83][84][85] The copious resources poured into product endorsement, placement, and other influencer marketing techniques across the spectrum of physical and digital domains trace their roots to these sociological effects.

81 Rogers, E. M. (2010). *Diffusion of innovations*. Simon and Schuster.

82 Rogers, E. M., & Shoemaker, F. F. (1971). Communication of Innovations; A Cross-Cultural Approach.

83 Kee, K. F. (2017). Adoption and diffusion. *The international encyclopedia of organizational communication*, 1-14.

84 Berliner, R. M., Hardman, S., & Tal, G. (2019). Uncovering early adopter's perceptions and purchase intentions of automated vehicles: Insights from early adopters of electric vehicles in California. *Transportation research part F: traffic psychology and behaviour, 60*, 712-722.

85 Kalantari, M., & Rauschnabel, P. (2018). Exploring the early adopters of augmented reality smart glasses: The case of Microsoft HoloLens. *In Augmented reality and virtual reality* (pp. 229-245). Springer, Cham.

Dating to at least the ancient Greeks, recorded tension between idea merit and persuasion exists. Socrates argued for the integrity of merit — an idea should stand on its own for quality and the best way to understand merit is through self-discovery. The Socratic method and its use of stimulated questioning is a companion technique to this thinking.

A lesser known group, the sophists, stood in contrast to Socrates and argued that persuasion is the ultimate achievement. The Sophists were more concerned with being able to convince others that a particular opinion was to be believed or idea embraced — even if the underlying value or approach was unfounded or flawed. Whereas Socrates was concerned only with merit–even when it wasn't something he wanted to believe.

With little effort it's likely you can come up with examples of people with brilliant ideas who have a hard time persuading other to embrace them. It's also likely you can quickly think of people can persuade others, but who often do so by saying whatever will serve their purposes.

The power of advocacy harnesses the relevant and worthy elements of both–allegiance to merit and self-discovery and skillful but only truthful persuasion — while shedding their negative elements. The result is increased odds for idea adoption through skillfully engaging advocates who help to spur broader adoption from those more likely to follow an idea's influential supporters than the idea itself.

Abner Portillo, a regional manager for the world's then largest independent oil and gas exploration and production company employed the advocate approach to win adoption for a reduced oil package size to serve the Central America region (and beyond). Despite having solid validation for the idea through a series of simple experiments and strong documented interest from target consumers, his first attempt to sell the idea (going it alone) received little interest from the home office.

So, he changed his method and enlisted the help of a well-regarded executive. He carefully walked her through the benefits of the idea — and the risks to ignoring it. He outlined what he'd learned from his initial validation efforts. Convinced of the idea's value, she shared it with a few other influential people in the firm whom agreed to voice their support for the new approach. Together Portillo and this executive again pitched the idea to the home office, citing references from the other managers. This time the home office embraced the idea, which went on to significantly influence how the firm conducted business not only in Central America but also in other emerging markets, globally.

Working with advocates requires the willingness to allow others to participate early and substantively in an idea. But fear of losing control or credit, among other factors, often keep people from sharing. Often keep people from sharing — leaving them with the words "I had that idea first" as a hollow consolation when the idea later takes root elsewhere.

Like the spark before a flame, even the best ideas can be fragile and need to be nurtured through the adoption process. Recognizing that ideas are more likely to gain traction when advocates are involved provides the motivation to overcome control or credit hesitations. And, knowing how to involve advocates in particular ways provides the strategic understanding to advance ideas forward.

IDENTIFYING ADVOCATES

When selecting advocates two characteristics are essential. First, the advocate must be perceived as influential (have the ability to affect others' actions). The advocate must also have sufficient interest in the idea to invest the effort and goodwill to understand and associate with it (the time and desire to learn about and, potentially, promote the idea).

Consider the video of idea adoption organically unfolding at music festival to understand the power of advocates in action. The video begins with an individual from the crowd beginning to dance in an open space of grass among the concert-goers. Of the relevant three minutes of footage nearly the first quarter shows this man dancing alone.

Just as it becomes painful to watch this man persist alone, another concert-goer joins him. The original dancer receives the advocate warmly and quickly involves him in the dancing. Within seconds of mirroring the original person's dance moves, the advocate makes a hand gesture to what we learn are his friends who quickly emerge from out of frame to join the original two dancers. One lone dancer is now a small group.

The initial group soon draws the attention of more casual onlookers who increasingly venture to join them. Before long, it becomes riskier to be left out than to join in the dancing and a large crowd takes shape. In just a few minutes the scene transforms from a lone individual awkwardly dancing alone to a full social movement around that individual's original idea.

Upon further review, without the advocate it's unlikely the originator's 'idea' would have been adopted. The advocate provided the initial group that affiliation coverage they needed to join in.

Advocates don't commit their influence lightly. Their interest needs to be peaked through the idea's merit and benefits, but then they are able to activate others to build the beginnings of a movement around the idea. Whether digitally or physically, the social science underpinnings for idea adoption are constant.

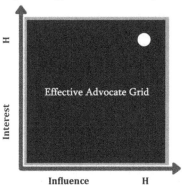

Figure 17   **Effective Advocate Grid**

Exhibit 17 highlights key interest and influence indicators to consider when seeking and engaging advocates.

Exhibit 18   Effective Advocate Indicators

interest

mindset

Does this person show interest in innovative thinking?	
Is this person willing to stand out?	
Does this person focus on learning and growth?	

resources

Does this person have the required time available?	
Is this person likely to understand the concept?	
Does this person follow through?	

goodwill

Does person volunteer to take on new initiatives?	
Does this person have an incentive to help?	
Will this person attach his/her reputation to the idea?	

influence

standing

Is this person respected?	
Does this person have meaningful authority?	
Can this person quickly tap a relevant network?	

credibility

Is this person perceived to be qualified?	
Does this person have skills relevant to the initiative?	
Do others turn to this person for help?	

integrity

Is this person perceived to be fair?	
Is this person perceived to be thoughtful?	
Does this person do what s/he says?	

Discovery section ⟶

Part I: Respond

Respond to the questions below using the following rating scale:
A = Always.   B = Often.   C = Sometimes.   D = Rarely.   E = Never.

32. I seek the aid of advocates to win adoption
    for ideas?

33. I seek out advocates who are high in interest
    and influence?

34. I go it alone when seeking adoption for
    my ideas?

Part II: Describe

For the following questions, describe how you would most likely respond.
To get the most from your efforts, **don't** describe what you *think you should
do*, but rather *what you would most likely actually do* based on how you've
responded to similar situations in the past.

**Your idea has validated well and is ready to get others on board.
How do you go about this?**

Suggested responses to Part I: A, A, E

167

How would you like your innovation approach to improve for having reviewed this chapter's insights? If you were asked to explain to others the power of "Messengers," what would you share?

Practice Activities Section

Choose an idea you consider to be promising, but you've not yet won its adoption.

Step #1 — Think of an idea you'd like to get adopted. Who do you think would make a good advocate to help you win adoption?

What will make them interested?

_____

_____

_____

_____

What influence does this person enjoy that you'd like to access?

_____

_____

_____

_____

_____

In what ways could you raise their interest in employing their influence?

_____

_____

_____

_____

_____

_____

_____

DISCOVERY SECTION

Step #2 — Envision how you would engage this advocate and describe what you envision here. What concerns do you anticipate s/he may have? How could you overcome these obstacles? What incentives should you consider? How could you harness incentives important to this advocate to advance the idea?

_____

_____

_____

_____

_____

_____

_____

_____

_____

_____

_____

_____

_____

_____

_____

_____

_____

_____

_____

_____

_____

_____

_____

_____

_____

The value of an insight is found in its doing. What are at least two concrete actions that can help you to more consistently engage "Messengers?"

_____

_____

_____

_____

_____

_____

_____

_____

_____

What benefit(s) do you anticipate from doing these actions well?

_____

_____

_____

_____

_____

_____

_____

_____

_____

_____

_____

_____

_____

12.

MESSAGES

Messages can help to shape perception. And, perception significantly influences action. Consider a simple experiment with drinking water.

People from various walks of life are presented two options. One is an elegant looking, European-branded bottle filled with regular tap water. The other is an unmarked bottle filled with more expensive, higher quality mountain stream-purified water. Participants are asked to drink the water from each container and select which they think is the higher quality.

The majority select the poorer quality water housed in the elegantly branded bottle. Why?

Their *perception* of quality (influenced by the bottles' packaging) overshadows the reality of what they're experiencing. They think the elegantly branded water *should* taste better, so in that split second between experience and response they convince themselves that it does. A second layer to the experiment reinforces this point. Without revealing the results from the first test, participants are presented a second chance to distinguish the water quality — but this time only unmarked bottles are used for both options. Presented this way, the majority accurately select the mountain stream-purified water.

In the first round, peoples' perception of what they think *should be* blinds them to the reality of *what really is* — a distinction they clearly identify in the second round. This example highlights important insights into the role perception can play in influencing ideas that gain adoption from those that don't. While humans will always have varied preferences, the job of messaging is to give the idea the opportunity to be openly assessed.

While humans will always have varied preferences, the job of messaging is to give the idea the opportunity to be candidly considered. To do this, it's important to recognize how personal interests and audience bias can skew exchanges and derail adopting otherwise worthy ideas.[86][87] Effective messaging helps to cut through these potential inhibitors and increases the odds that the idea will be viewed openly.

MESSAGE QUALITY

The message used to convey an idea largely determines whether advocates will support the idea and how well it translates to broader audiences. More effective messages blend persuasion and merit.[88][89] They contain five important characteristics.

REFINED

Messages evolve in three stages. The first is simplistic. In this stage, the message is largely assumptive and shows a lack of rigorous inquiry. It is easily rejected by a discerning audience.

---

86   Chung, M. (2019). The message influences me more than others: How and why social media metrics affect first person perception and behavioral intentions. *Computers in Human Behavior, 91*, 271–278.

87   Desmidt, S., & Heene, A. (2007). Mission statement perception: Are we all on the same wavelength? A case study in a Flemish hospital. *Health Care Management Review, 32*(1), 77–87.

88   Heath, C., & Heath, D. (2007). *Made to stick: Why some ideas survive and others die.* Random House.

89   Schwarz, N., Newman, E., & Leach, W. (2016). Making the truth stick & the myths fade: Lessons from cognitive psychology. *Behavioral Science & Policy, 2*(1), 85–95.

The second is complex. In this stage, the message tries to convey everything related to the idea, but lacks relevance and focus. Complexity is an important step beyond the simplistic stage because it treats the idea more deeply and broadly, but it fails to distill the information to its most relevant form. It is like developing a large strategic plan without being able to succinctly describe its pathway forward.

Effective messages push through complexity to emerge with a storyline that is refined (simple and precise). Consider the mission statement from Microsoft's early days when the objective was to make personal computing ubiquitous, *"There will be a personal computer on every desk running Microsoft software."* After hearing the message just once the audience can appreciate its value and convey the same to others with at least 80% accuracy.

PERSONAL

None of the message elements that follow will matter if recipients don't believe you understand what is meaningful to them. Even when intended for larger audiences the goal is to leave each person with the impression–*they get me*. By beginning with the question, "why does this matter to the recipient?" and working forward the temptation to cloud agendas is reduced. Effective Bridgers diagnose their audience's interests and the roots of potential resistance before trying to persuade.

Part of why Shakespeare's *Macbeth* endures is people from nearly every station in life can find themselves in his work. By anchoring to genuine human condition themes (among them, hope for a better future) even large, diverse groups of people can relate to the message on a personal level. The "see yourself in a Honda" campaign was a contemporary adaptation of this technique. To be personal, messages understand the target audience intimately and speak directly to their interests. When this is not possible, they anchor to widely held human desires and invite the audience to see themselves in the message.

EMOTIONAL

Feelings influence actions. Emerging neuroscience notes that emotions are essential for choosing.[90] [91] [92] For example, otherwise normal people with damage in the part of the brain where emotions are generated demonstrate tremendous difficulty making decisions. They can describe in logical terms what should be done, but they cannot act on that logic. This phenomenon extends to even basic decisions, such as what clothes to wear. Without the emotional function to aid decision making, these subjects could not arrive at a decision.

Those who raise money for social causes have long understood the importance of emotion to motivate giving. For example, people are significantly less likely to give when appealed to by numbers alone compared to the story of a single child. Regardless of the theme, effectively embedding emotion into a message gets people to suspend their critical selves for a period so they can feel; they get people to associate with things they care about or appeal to their personal interests.

CONCRETE

Contrast two approaches from a global healthcare company to promote their wellness program. The first described the many health benefits from using their program, including: weight loss, potential cholesterol reduction, and decreased blood pressure. That campaign had limited success and was unceremoniously canceled.

Their next approach gained far more traction. Three simple visuals were represented with verbal prompts, "From *this* (featuring the image of someone overweight) to *this* (the next image featured the

---

90 Zalocusky, K. A., Ramakrishnan, C., Lerner, T. N., Davidson, T. J., Knutson, B., & Deisseroth, K. (2016). Nucleus accumbens D2R cells signal prior outcomes and control risky decision-making. *Nature, 531*(7596), 642–646.

91 Damasio, A., & Carvalho, G. B. (2013). The nature of feelings: evolutionary and neurobiological origins. *Nature Reviews Neuroscience, 14*(2), 143–152.

92 Bechara, A., Damasio, H., & Damasio, A. R. (2000). Emotion, decision making and the orbitofrontal cortex. *Cerebral cortex, 10*(3), 295–307.

same person after losing the weight) for *this* (the final image featured that person in an active social setting with family and friends).

Both messages pulled from the same information, but the second one resonated more profoundly. Using concrete examples turns abstract concepts (like cholesterol) into something relatable. Relevant stories, metaphors, and everyday analogies are effective ways to help an audience make sense of a new idea.

CREDIBLE

Message credibility derives largely from three sources: authority, empirical data and statistics, and testable assertions. Authority is attributed power to influence opinions and behavior. Professional credentials, previous experiences and expertise, and social status are common ways authority is built and harnessed. Messages delivered from a position of authority tend to reduce skepticism.

When authority is not available, anti-authority can serve as proxy. Rather than stating a message is credible because it derives from an authority figure's thoughts or example, the anti-authority approach is more widely available and describes what not to do. For example, while only an oncologist can speak from a position of authority to the advances in cancer treatment anyone who has been affected by cancer (whether or not personally) can speak to which treatments were more or less effective. Apple used a savvy twist to the anti-authority message technique in their "Get a Mac" campaign that painted the PC user as out of touch and the Apple user as hip and the counter-norm.

Empirical data and statistics build credibility by supporting a message's emotional elements with objective findings. They help the audience to rationally connect the dots between need and solution and help to overcome the single-case temptation (one occurrence presented as a trend).

How statistics are reported is important. Concrete examples give form to statistics that might otherwise be overlooked. Stating that nearly 50% of people in Africa live below the poverty line is less memorable than describing that if Africa were a family of four either the parents or the children wouldn't get enough to eat–ever. While both examples present the same data, the latter is likely to have stronger impact.

Another valuable message technique to build credibility is to encourage the audience to test validity for themselves. For example, when KIA Motors wanted to build credibility for what was then an under known and economy-level positioned brand in North America, they introduced the 100,000 warranty. The implicit message was that KIA really stands behind the quality of their vehicles and they're worth considering.[93][94]

Testable assertions give the audience power to understand for themselves a message's value. This is precisely what former U.S. president Ronald Reagan did when he asked voters during a pivotal election debate, "are you better off today than you were four years ago?"[95]

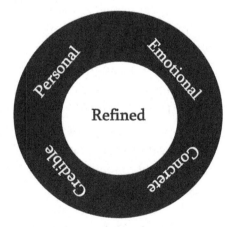

Exhibit 19   **Effective Message Characteristics**

---

93   https://www.kia.com/us/en/warranty. Retrieved June 13, 2020.

94   Southerton, D. G. (2012). *Hyundai and Kia motors: The early years and product development*. Don Southerton.

95   https://www.youtube.com/watch?v=I6Eb-ynLMrs. Retrieved June 6, 2020.
    Discovery section →

Part I: Respond

Respond to the questions below using the following rating scale:
A = Always.   B = Often.   C = Sometimes.   D = Rarely.   E = Never.

35. I systematically develop my message before trying to win an idea's adoption?

36. Messages I develop include personalization, emotion, concreteness, and credibility?

37. My messages are refined?

Part II: Describe

For the following questions, describe how you would most likely respond. To get the most from your efforts, **don't** describe what you *think you should do*, but rather *what you would most likely actually do* based on how you've responded to similar situations in the past.

Your idea has validated well and is ready to get others on board. You identify an advocate and are asked to prepare and send over a brief overview that builds the case for your idea. How do you go about this?

How would you like your innovation approach to improve for having reviewed this chapter's insights? If you were asked to explain to others what makes for great "Messages," what would you share?

Practice Activities Section

Choose an idea you consider to be promising. Utilize the five key attributes discussed to develop a message likely to win advocate support for your idea.

PERSONAL — Who is your audience and what are their interests?

_____

_____

_____

EMOTIONAL — How can you gain their attention by tapping into hope/fear emotions?

_____

_____

_____

CONCRETE — What examples or analogies can you use to increase your audience's understanding of the idea's benefit?

_____

_____

_____

CONCRETE — What examples or analogies can you use to increase your audience's understanding of the idea's benefit?

_____

_____

_____

REFINED — What about your message ensures someone hearing it for the first time can repeat its key points with at least 80% accuracy?

_____

_____

_____

DISCOVERY SECTION

Step #2 — Put these elements together to write a succinct message that builds a strong case for your idea.

The value of an insight is found in its doing. What are at least two concrete actions that can help you to develop high-impact "Messages?"

_____

_____

_____

_____

_____

_____

_____

_____

What benefit(s) do you anticipate from doing these actions well?

_____

_____

_____

_____

_____

_____

_____

_____

_____

_____

_____

_____

13

BUILDING BRIDGER SKILLS IN OTHERS

Voted European Player of the 20th century (and second only to Pelé for World Player of the Century), Dutch footballer Johan Cruyff is widely credited with revolutionizing how the contemporary game is played. From advancing the *total football* position-fluid playing strategy to signature moves now firmly embedded in the game, like the 'Cruyff Turn,' few players made a larger imprint on the world's most popular sport than Johan.

Of Cruyff famous English striker Gary Lineker described, "(He) did more to make the beautiful game beautiful than anyone in history."[96]

His playing career stellar, Cruyff's coaching career was similarly extraordinary. While some greats struggle to move from player to mentor, Cruyff made the transition seamlessly. On the pitch, he was among the best in the world — winning three Ballon d'Or designations (the highest individual honor, globally) and willing his national team to finishes most experts believe far outstripped their standing in world soccer. As a coach, Cruyff led Dutch club Ajax

---

96   "Gary Lineker: 'Sad to hear that Johan Cruyff has died. Football has lost a man who did more to make the beautiful game beautiful than anyone in history.'" Twitter.com 24 March 2016. Retrieved March 10, 2019.

and Spanish club Barcelona to the sport's pinnacle while infusing the clubs with new-age tactics and player development well before their time. In total, Cruyff coached clubs won two European Cups, 2 Cup Winners' Cup, four La Liga Championships, five domestic cups and one UEFA Super Cup. Along the way he pioneered innovation that changed the game for good and developed the same capacity in others.

Of the wisdom Cruyff shared before his passing, few insights are sager than, "Speed is often confused with insight. When I start running earlier than the others, I appear faster. You need to look, you need to think, you need to move, you need to find space, you need to help others."[97] This ethos served Cruyff well as he transitioned from world-class player to player developer.

It can be tempting to view innovation capacity as born rather than built. Research and practical experience strongly indicate otherwise.[98] [99] [100] [101] Bridger skills can be sharpened in anyone willing to make the effort. Thriving as a Bridger yourself builds appreciation for the approach and credibility with others. And, embracing best practice for developing Bridgers amplifies the potential for impact well beyond your own efforts.

Five keys make the difference.

97   Oyesiku, N. M. (2016). Johan Cruyff (1947–2016). *Neurosurgery, 79*(1), 1–2.

98   Dyer, J., Gregersen, H., & Christensen, C. M. (2019). *Innovator's DNA, Updated, with a New Preface: Mastering the Five Skills of Disruptive Innovators.* Harvard Business Press.

99   Tuzovic, S., Wirtz, J., & Heracleous, L. (2018). How do innovators stay innovative? A longitudinal case analysis. *Journal of Services Marketing, 32*(1), 34–45.

100   Wisnioski, M., Hintz, E. S., Kleine, M. S., Fasihuddin, H., Cavagnaro, L. B., McManus, M., ... & Godin, B. (2019). 19 Remaking the Innovator Imperative.

101   Rivet, D. J. (2017). Amazon's Superior Innovation: A Study of Amazon's corporate structure, CEO, and reasons behind why it has become the most innovative company in today's market.

SET THE TONE

Change may be inevitable — as the former U.S. Army Chief of Staff Eric Shinseki famously remarked "If you dislike change, you're going to dislike irrelevance even more" — but as legitimacy comes easier through looking and acting like others the most needed change can be difficult to sponsor and embrace. Innovation is the critical mechanism for achieving a particular change. For others to venture beyond the safety of conformity, the tone must be set that effective innovation is both encouraged and expected.

ENCOURAGED

Encouragement (inspiring support, confidence, or hope) is both personal and interpersonal — and they tend to work together. Think of when you feel encouraged. For most, the thrill of opportunity is present. There is hope that tomorrow will be better than today, and their actions are critical for that better tomorrow. This ideally comes from within.

But encouragement is also social. Systems, language, and actions build or diminish encouragement. For example, below are five encouragement hinderances:

- Overly helping or domineering
- Negatively comparing someone to others
- Setting standards that can't be reasonably met
- Goodwill consuming by primarily sharing in first-person
- Providing defeatist or unfounded outlooks

Encouragement also positively influences performance. Not even elite athletes are immune to the effects of positive and negative encouragement. The research highlights that athletes, both women and men, perform significantly better when they are encouraged. While their physical attributes are the same, their ability to unleash their best output is influenced by whether they think others around them believe in their potential.[102] [103] This is consistent with broader neurological research; when we're encouraged, the areas of our brain that help us with creativity and cognitive thinking light up.[104] [105]

Global mining company Rio Tinto (among others) used the term *social license to operate* extensively during our work together. This is to have the willful approval and support of the local communities and stakeholders where they operate. Encouragement provides a similar *license to operate* for those around us; permission to think and act innovatively.

EXPECTED

Expectations give teeth to encouragement. Together, encouragement and expectation are the the strong belief that someone can achieve something and the invitation to do so. Building Bridgers includes the expectation that others can and should contribute great ideas — and explicitly sharing this expectation with them.

Enterprise hallways and boardrooms the world over are lined with imagery encouraging innovation. But if the one-to-one interactions, systems, and informal organization don't reinforce and support these expectations, they become caricatures — symbols to shallow intent.

Great expectations embody three elements: objectives, timing, and incentives.

The best objectives are wise: worthwhile (meaningful), integrated (congruent with other key activities), specific (easily

102 McCormick, A., Meijen, C., & Marcora, S. (2015). Psychological determinants of whole-body endurance performance. *Sports medicine, 45*(7), 997–1015.

103 Andreacci, J. L., Lemura, L. M., Cohen, S. L., Urbansky, E. A., Chelland, S. A., & Duvillard, S. P. V. (2002). The effects of frequency of encouragement on performance during maximal exercise testing. *Journal of sports sciences, 20*(4), 345–352.

104 Rogers, E., & van Dam, N. (2015). *You the Positive Force In Change: Leveraging Insights from Neuroscience and Positive Psychology.* Lulu Press, Inc.

105 Daniel, G., & Goleman, D. (2006). Social Intelligence: The New Science of Human Relationships. *Bantam Dell Pub Group.*

understood), and executable (possible with available resources). They clearly outline the desired outcome's relevance to those involved within existing priorities and available resources.

Leadership at Adelca, one of South America's premier steel manufacturer's, harnessed wise objectives to organize the informal scrap metal effort in Ecuador. Facing a shortage of input material to meet the demand for their manufacturing operations, the call was put out to develop ideas that would power the company's next growth wave while reducing dependence on external sources. Bridgers in the company saw the opportunity to repurpose the country's significant supply of scrap metal and pioneer a recycling movement.

This required Bridgers to innovate incentives and reliable systems for thousands of informal workers and small to medium-sized providers to work with the company and accumulate the scrap piece by piece, and pile by pile.[106] The resulting *Recyclers Club* changed for good not only Adelca's supply chain, but also fueled upward mobility for thousands of workers. Working with their executive team over the years, it is clear that this and subsequent innovation were born of leadership's willingness to set the tone by building the expectation that Bridgers can and should exist throughout their ranks and consistently encouraging Bridgers' best efforts. This contributes to a seize-each-moment ethos.

The safety allure of *when, then* thinking — when conditions become ideal, then desired actions will be taken — keeps many would-be innovators from seizing the present. In dynamic operating environments, however, conditions are never perfect; they're fluid by definition — so a self-imposed paralysis takes effect. Conditions tend to improve as action is taken, not the other way around.[107] Timeliness expectations turn the *when, then* temptation into *now, not then* invitations.

---

106 Conaway, J. (2015) Forging Value from Scrap. Inter-American Development Bank.

107 van Eerde, W., & Klingsieck, K. B. (2018). Overcoming procrastination? A meta-analysis of intervention studies. *Educational Research Review, 25*, 73–85.

Clear incentives complete the expectations triad. A primary fear of would-be innovators is their ideas will be taken if shared. This overvalues the role of ideas and undervalues the importance of execution, but highlights the perception that would-be innovators quickly assign their ideas emotional and monetary value. Effectively building Bridger behavior embraces this understanding.

While incentive applications vary by type of enterprise, industry norms, and broader economic conditions, proven commonalities include: authorship credit, potential for a leading role in the idea's build-out, potential for upward mobility, potential impact-driven bonus systems, and implementation resources.

ADVANCE THE SKILL

Encouragement and expectations without competence-building are frustrating. Advancing skills is aided by 1) accurately assessing the current skillset 2) embracing best practice development journeys to sharpen Bridger competencies.

Organizations need to understand the competency starting-point for would-be Bridgers and actively invest in further developing Bridgers' skills. Assessment tools can help leaders predict suitability for Bridger work, initially, and measure the impact from Bridger development over time. Having a clear sense for what distinguishes successful Bridgers from others is a great place to start.

Effective Bridgers are able to do the following:[108]

- Exhibit an innovator's mindset
- Quickly develop trusting relationships both internally (with advocates) and externally
- Demonstrate knowledge of current business models
- Intentional observation by building-a-bigger-box
- Develop valuable connections between observations and opportunities

---

108 Hunsaker, B. T. (2020). Innovation Bridgers: The new talent imperative. *Thunderbird International Business Review, 62*(4), 385–392.

- Show creativity by designing quick, inexpensive experiments to test ideas
- Excel in less-familiar environments
- Understand how to win acceptance for new ideas

CREATE THE SPACE

During a meeting with the executive development head for one of the world's largest and legacy materials science companies, he shared his perceived disconnect between what the company asked of its people verbally and symbolically (mission statements, slogans, and office imagery), and reality. Innovation was encouraged, but rewards reinforced incremental revenue and profit output. Their performance reviews and performance metrics spoke of innovation, but related time, training, and resources were less forthcoming. Status often trumped idea merit. Acquiescence was better received than genuine questions. Stronger outcomes were called for, but risk tacitly discouraged. A culture of saying one thing, but reinforcing another had taken root.

Innovation is the mechanism for purposeful change. Considering better ways of operating, models, and direction requires the willingness to step into new territory; to examine and, perhaps, depart from current norms. This has far less to do with physical space, and more to do with addressing social, political, and emotional barriers. To be sure there will be challenges and, even, missteps along the way. But allowing Bridgers' space for some things to go manageably wrong is essential to allow for the possibility of gamechanger insights going very right.[109][110][111]

---

109 Eskreis-Winkler, L., & Fishbach, A. (2019). Not learning from failure—The greatest failure of all. *Psychological science, 30*(12), 1733–1744.

110 Edmondson, A. C. (2011). Strategies for learning from failure. *Harvard business review, 89*(4), 48–55.

111 Storey, J., & Barnett, E. (2000). Knowledge management initiatives: learning from failure. *Journal of knowledge management.*

Ways to create space include:

- Communicate that risk-taking is important
- Encourage curiosity and meaningful questioning
- Model intentions through actions
- Ask for input before sharing to limit authority bias
- Provide time to develop relationships and ideate
- Make Bridger activities an explicit part of job descriptions
- Ensure what is measured invites innovation
- Supply consistent, accessible outlets for new ideas to be shared
- Support the best ideas regardless of their source

SUPPORT THE PROCESS

Support systems and resources give fuel to the space created. It is too common for organizations to not have a clearly defined process for openly scouting and adopting innovation beyond formal R&D teams. Based on the success of Bridger Abner Portillo (smaller package innovation) and others, ConocoPhillips moved to formally tracking ideas through its best practices portal to encourage other Bridgers to do what Portillo did. Creating a system to capture and share emerging innovations demonstrates the company's commitment to finding and supporting great new ideas, regardless of their source, and facilitates the process of integrating ideas into the home office.

Because business continuity and innovation require distinct efforts and risk tolerances, Bayer AG (the German pharmaceutical and life-science giant), has a separate mandate to distinguish the two aimed to harness the ingenuity of the entire enterprise. Monika Lessel, Head of Corporate Innovation, R&D, and Societal Engagement for Bayer describes, "Innovation is at our core to be responsive to (constituent) needs. We strive to tap into our full innovation potential of more than 100,000 employees across Bayer.

Innovation fuels tomorrow's impact, which is why it is critical that we enable and empower an entrepreneurial spirit across Bayer today."[112]

To support this process and complement the firm's in-house R&D efforts, Bayer resources deep-dive 360 stakeholder engagement and localized open innovation platforms. The platforms are reviewed by innovation advocates for promising concepts (in collaboration with idea originators), with the best further stress tested for commercialization promise. Tracing systems ensure self-directed idea attribution–encouraging open sharing. The company continuously cultivates a relevant funnel of promising concepts that are de-risked through further validation and, ultimately, resourced for launch or unwound. These actions convey alignment between the firm's intentions, communications, and supporting processes.

Leaders who actively identify and groom Bridger skills in others—and structure organizations to invite and maximize the insights Bridger's provide—will have an advantage. Rather than using the Bridger strategy to solve a specific problem, firms need to integrate the strategy into their normal ways of doing business so that they are prepared to find and develop innovations in unfamiliar environments. Distinguishing standard from bridger-supportive approaches provides the foundation from which to build.

---

112 https://www.bayer.com/en/research-and-innovation.aspx. Retrieved August 15, 2020.

	The Standard Process	The Bridger Strategy
How Bridgers scout for ideas	Managers focus on push approaches; their line of sight is to implement existing strategies. The firm emphasizes uncovering information that supports its current operating practices or meets the needs of the most vocal of its existing customers. Managers rely on aggregated studies or customer surveys.	Bridgers line of sight has dual purpose—to implement strategies and to discover ideas that could improve the organization's position. Through observation and relationship building and bigger-box-building, bridgers gain intimate access to local environments and connect insights to opportunities.
How managers filter ideas	Managers scrub and sanitize ideas before presenting them to leaders, especially if their suggestions are controversial or threaten existing organizational practices. There is little to no incentive to involve internal and external colleagues in teasing out ideas.	Managers recognize that valuable new ideas can be both opportunities and threats to organizational structures. Before presenting new ideas to senior managers, bridgers test the soundness and relevance of their recommendations by working with translators to conduct simple experiments in the field.
How ideas gain acceptance	Consideration of new ideas is a low priority, despite communication to the contrary, and is usually trumped by immediate operational activities. It takes a long time for leaders to consider ideas. This lag time reduces ideas' likelihood of being implemented, regardless of their strategic merit.	Bridgers present ideas expeditiously, according to a clear process and in concrete language, having considered initial validation. Managers approve the best ideas based on their strategic merit and quickly implement them.
How teams implement ideas	If an idea makes it through, the firm pulls resources for it from existing business units and initially considers it a "side project." Teams are rewarded for preserving their budgets rather than risking a new, most likely competitive, model.	The firm sets aside resources to fund the best ideas and communicates their value internally and externally. Bridgers often participate in teams' implementation of their ideas to ensure that they match bridgers' original intentions.

Exhibit 20   **Contrasting the Standard & Bridger Approaches**

CELEBRATE EARLY WINS

The adage, 'input quality is an important outcome in itself' reminds leaders to celebrate process milestones –not just the ultimate result. Bridger's are more likely to persist through challenges and resistance (and consistently look beyond their own office walls and aggregated reports) if early wins are effectively recognized. At least three milestones can be celebrated by enterprises from all industries or development cycles. Think of these as key layers to a progress recognition funnel.

EFFECTIVE IDEATION

Seeing valuable opportunities that others miss is an enterprise's lifeblood. But no operational acumen can compensate for poor idea input. Bridgers are critical sources for staying abreast of high-growth opportunities. Yet, by the numbers only a small minority of an organization's personnel engages in effective ideation — let alone the other aspects of being an effective Bridger. Some of this is due to idea-stifling cultures. Another part can be attributed to the lack of professional development for effective ideation and validation skills. The rest comes from distrust that ideas will be appropriately recognized and rewarded; skepticism that the effort is worthwhile. These barriers are largely reduced when effective ideation is personally and publicly celebrated.

Recognition mechanisms are best when they befit a given enterprise. But in all circumstances the common elements are tailoring to acknowledge the individual's interest and contribution and a method for public idea attribution. The latter has the added benefit of signaling to others that effectively scouted and initially validated ideas will be valued and respected.

WINNING ADOPTION

It is quite possible that a gamechanger idea for any given firm is sitting in one of its own offices somewhere.[113] One thing is to scout a valuable idea. Another is to get it noticed. Both are needed.

By the data we know that if we can encourage people to initially validate their ideas, the likelihood of them sharing their better ideas skyrockets. When paired with messenger strategy savvy and messaging skills, the odds for that idea winning adoption also shoot up (these odds rise even more for enterprises with effective idea support systems).

Post-ideation, but pre-implementation, is the second opportunity to celebrate an early win. Among the flood of ideas, this

---

113 https://hbr.org/2012/01/finding-great-ideas-in-emergin. Retrieved February 10, 2020.

milestone recognizes those ideas (and their contributors) that stood out as worthy of resourcing for implementation. Just as the middle-funnel strategy is crucial to a sales cycle, so too is celebrating when Bridger ideas win adoption.

SUCCESSFUL IMPLEMENTATION

It is little wonder that some universities excel at faculty-led discovery and innovation resulting in commercial success and others lag despite tremendously capable talent and funding inflows. This is largely attributed to systems that catalyze or stifle successful implementation. For example, Stanford University promotes a system of shared benefit (commensurate with risk and resourcing). Many of their peers spend their best efforts limiting faculty interests.[114]

The same is found in other sectors. To be sure some industries require creativity beyond monetary gain (e.g. government agencies), but all are better served when Bridgers are appropriately recognized for successfully implemented ideas.

By the implementation phase an idea has traveled quite the journey, spanning initial observation to go-to-market (or go-to-operation for non-commercial ideas) resourcing and launch, and all of the phases and challenges in between. Standing up these success cases, and their originators, is key to encouraging more of the same.

CONCLUSION

As operating environments grow more dynamic the need for people who effectively scout new opportunities, test them for viability, and skillfully win their adoption increases. Not all ideas are valuable. Bridgers understand this and engage specific techniques to uncover new advantages. With limited time and capital, they

---

114 Sanberg, P. R., Gharib, M., Harker, P. T., Kaler, E. W., Marchase, R. B., Sands, T. D., ... & Sarkar, S. (2014). Changing the academic culture: Valuing patents and commercialization toward tenure and career advancement. *Proceedings of the National Academy of Sciences, 111*(18), 6542–6547.

conduct initial validation tests to filter for ideas worthy of further attention and resources. They then embrace specific approaches to win the idea's adoption.

Building Bridger skills in others begins with your own actions. Insert yourself in the Bridger role. Select an industry (or segment within that industry) of interest and identify a valuable new idea that can shape it for good going forward. Initially validate your hypothesis. Outline an effective advocate strategy for the idea and develop a compelling message to win advocate interest.

Then do it again — empowering others to do the same.

Discovery section →

Part I: Respond

Respond to the questions below using the following rating scale:

A = Always.   B = Often.   C = Sometimes.   D = Rarely.   E = Never.

38. I encourage and expect others to become Bridgers?

39. I actively help others to develop their Bridger skills?

40. I promote systems that support Bridger action success?

Part II: Describe

For the following questions, describe how you would most likely respond. To get the most from your efforts, **don't** describe what you *think you should do*, but rather *what you would most likely actually do* based on how you've responded to similar situations in the past.

You're asked to broaden and deepen your organization's innovation efforts. What do you emphasize?

How would you like your innovation approach to improve for having reviewed this chapter's insights? If you were asked to explain to others how to "Build Bridger Skills in Others," what would you share?

Practice Activities Section

Think of someone you believe shows promise to further develop their Bridger skills. Briefly game plan the development foundation. In addition to the individual, you'll also consider the role of support systems.

Step #1 — How could help them at the individual level?

What Bridger competency strengths does this person have to build on?

_____

_____

_____

_____

What skills need further development?

_____

_____

_____

_____

_____

What encouragement and expectations would you provide?

_____

_____

_____

_____

_____

Step #2 — How could you help to navigate and/or provide catalytic systems?

How can you help to create space for this person?

_____

_____

_____

_____

_____

_____

_____

How can you tangibly improve the process for this person?

_____

_____

_____

_____

_____

_____

_____

In what ways do you envision celebrating early wins?

_____

_____

_____

_____

_____

_____

_____

The value of an insight is found in its doing. What are at least two concrete actions that can help you to more consistently "Build Others' Bridger Skills?"

_____

_____

_____

_____

_____

_____

_____

_____

_____

_____

_____

_____

_____

_____

_____

_____

_____

_____

_____

_____

_____

_____

_____

What benefit(s) do you anticipate from doing these actions well?

NOTES

CHAPTER 1

"Walmart". *Fortune*. Global 500. Retrieved August 12, 2019.

Washburn, N. T., & Hunsaker, B. T. (2011). Finding great ideas in emerging markets. *Harvard Business Review, 89*(9), 115–120.

https://www.youtube.com/watch?time_continue=60&v=tOOachJXSJM&feature=emb_titl Retrieved December 11, 2019.

CHAPTER 2

http://quickfacts.census.gov/qfd/states/06/0615044.html. Retrieved December 30, 2015.

https://www.youtube.com/watch?v=3K_4LfzKPko. Retrieved November 23, 2015.

Hunsaker, B. T. (2019) Autonomous University Strategy. Enterprising Capital.

BT. Hunsaker (2020) Innovation Bridgers: The new talent imperative. Thunderbird Int. Bus. Rev.

Singelis, T. M. (1994). The measurement of independent and interdependent self-construals. *Personality and Social Psychology Bulletin, 20*(5), 580–591.

Bouchard, T. J. and McGue, M. (2003), Genetic and environmental influences on human psychological differences. J. Neurobiol., 54: 4–45. doi: 10.1002/neu.10160

Yeager, D. S. & Dweck, C. S. (2012). Mindsets That Promote Resilience: When Students Believe That Personal Characteristics Can Be Developed. Educational Psychologist, 47(4), 302–314, 2012.

https://www.forbes.com/sites/andriacheng/2019/01/13/why-amazon-go-may-soon-change-the-way-we-want-to-shop/#4dbc86a76709 Retrieved May 26, 2019

https://www.forbes.com/sites/jonbird1/2019/04/14/bezos-on-amazon-just-a-small-player-in-global-retail/#2c556a8e4e76 Retrieved May 28, 2019

Takahashi, Dean, "How IBM Will Use Blockchain as its Commerce Backbone" Venture Beat, 08 September 2018 https://venturebeat.com/2018/09/08/how-ibm-will-use-blockchain-as-its-commerce-backbone/

Siebrase, Jamie. "Coda Coffee Co." CompanyWeek, 8 Jan. 2017; companyweek.com/company-profile/coda-coffee-co.

CHAPTER 3

Hunsaker, B. T. (2020) Innovation Bridgers: The new talent imperative. *Thunderbird International Business Review.*

Data compiled by the author during teaching experiments between 2011–2019 involving nearly 1,000 graduate students.

May 1997, World Wide Developers Conference (online video) 52:15/52:22

1961 June 5, New York Times, Edison Bust Enters Hall of Fame as Sarnoff Delivers a Eulogy, Quote Page 34, Column 7 and 8, New York.

Cooper, J. M., & Hutchinson, D. S. (Eds.). (1997). Plato: complete works. Hackett Publishing.

CHAPTER 4

Washburn, N., & Hunsaker, B. T. (2011). Finding great ideas in emerging markets.

von Hippel, W., & Suddendorf, T. (2018). Did humans evolve to innovate with a social rather than technical orientation?. *New Ideas in Psychology, 51,* 34–39.

Otto, A. R., Fleming, S. M., & Glimcher, P. W. (2016). Unexpected but incidental positive outcomes predict real-world gambling. *Psychological science,* 0956797615618366.

Hunsaker, BT (2018). Applied Learning — Social Proof of Mastery. Thunderbird Magazine.

http://www.glamour.com/inspired/2015/12/lindsey-stirling-highest-earning-female-youtuber. Retrieved December 9, 2015.

Jenkins, A. C., Dodell-Feder, D., Saxe, R., & Knobe, J. (2014). The Neural Bases of Directed and Spontaneous Mental State Attributions to Group Agents. *PloS one, 9*(8), e105341.

Saxe, R., & Young, L. (2013). Theory of Mind: How brains think about thoughts. *The handbook of cognitive neuroscience,* 204–213.

Bernhardt, B. C., & Singer, T. (2012). The neural basis of empathy. *Neuroscience, 35*(1), 1.

Saarela, M. V., Hlushchuk, Y., Williams, A. C. D. C., Schürmann, M., Kalso, E., & Hari, R. (2007). The compassionate brain: humans detect intensity of pain from another's face. *Cerebral cortex, 17*(1), 230–237.

Hunsaker, B.T. (2019) Mindset Positioning: Premier Development Edition.

Jenkins, A. C., Dodell-Feder, D., Saxe, R., & Knobe, J. (2014). The Neural Bases of Directed and Spontaneous Mental State Attributions to Group Agents. *PloS one, 9*(8), e105341.

Saxe, R., & Young, L. (2013). Theory of Mind: How brains think about thoughts. *The handbook of cognitive neuroscience,* 204–213.

Cooper, J. M., & Hutchinson, D. S. (Eds.). (1997). *Plato: complete works*. Hackett Publishing.

http://greatergood.berkeley.edu/raising_happiness/post/fake_it_till_you_make_it. Retrieved September 2, 2015.

CHAPTER 5
Leavy, B. (2016). Effective leadership today–character not just competence. *Strategy & Leadership*.

Simmons, J. (2012). *The Starbucks story: how the brand changed the world*. Marshall Cavendish International Asia Pte Ltd.

Schultz, H., & Gordon, J. (2012). *Onward: How Starbucks fought for its life without losing its soul*. Rodale books.

Koehn, N. F. (2001). Howard Schultz and Starbucks coffee company.

Rataul, P., Tisch, D. G., & Zámborský, P. (2018). *Netflix: Dynamic capabilities for global success*. SAGE Publications: SAGE Business Cases Originals.

Henry, C. (2018). Leadership and strategy in the news. *Strategy & Leadership*.

Grinapol, C. (2013). *Reed Hastings and Netflix*. The Rosen Publishing Group, Inc.

Farrow, R. (2012). Netflix heads into the clouds.

CHAPTER 6
https://www.sec.gov/Archives/edgar/data/1018724/000119312507093886/dex991.htm. Retrieved 12 May 2019

https://www.produceretailer.com/article/news-article/walmart-snagging-these-shoppers-grocery-pickup. Retrieved December 15, 2019.

https://www.warbyparker.com/. Retrieved June 4, 2019.

https://bonobos.com/ Retrieved June 7, 2019

NASDAQ: AMZN. Retrieved May 14, 2019.

wholefoodsmarket.com/news/amazon-and-whole-foods-market-announce-acquisition-to-close-this-monday-wil. Retrieved January 10, 2019.

https://www.investopedia.com/news/jeff-bezos-just-got-28-billion-richer-thanks-amazon-go/. Retrieved December 10, 2019.

https://www.cnbc.com/2019/04/12/amazons-jeff-bezos-most-us-sales-still-in-brick-and-mortar-stores.html. Retrieved December 2, 2019.

https://www.forbes.com/sits/andriacheng/2019/01/13/why-amazon-go-may-soon-change-the-way-we-want-to-shop/@4dbc86a76709. Retrieved May 26, 2019.

Showrav, D, & Nitu, R. (2018). The influence of brand equity on customer intention to pay premium price of the fashion house brand. *Management Science Letters*, *8*(12), 1291–1304.

Bıçakcıoğlu, N., Ögel, İ. Y., & İlter, B. (2017). Brand jealousy and willingness to pay premium: The mediating role of materialism. *Journal of brand Management, 24*(1), 33–48.

Li, G., Li, G., & Kambele, Z. (2012). Luxury fashion brand consumers in China: Perceived value, fashion lifestyle, and willingness to pay. *Journal of Business Research, 65*(10), 1516–1522.

Katz, J. E., & Sugiyama, S. (2006). Mobile phones as fashion statements: evidence from student surveys in the US and Japan. *New media & society, 8*(2), 321–337.

Caballero, R. J., Farhi, E., & Gourinchas, P. O. (2017). Rents, technical change, and risk premia accounting for secular trends in interest rates, returns on capital, earning yields, and factor shares. *American Economic Review, 107*(5), 614–20.

Tomaskovic-Devey, D., & Lin, K. H. (2011). Income dynamics, economic rents, and the financialization of the US economy. *American Sociological Review, 76*(4), 538–559.

Lado, A. A., Boyd, N. G., & Hanlon, S. C. (1997). Competition, cooperation, and the search for economic rents: A syncretic model. *Academy of management review, 22*(1), 110–141.

https://www.smh.com.au/business/companies/going-off-script-how-the-1-7b-bunnings-uk-disaster-unfolded-20180528-p4zhvw.html. Retrieved March 3, 2020.

Washburn, N., & Hunsaker, B. T. (2011). Finding great ideas in emerging markets. Harvard Business Review.

https://www.forbes.com/sites/patrickmoorhead/2018/03/21/intel-and-healthcare-partners-lean-into-ai-at-solve-event/#1d93b4de3d37. Retrieved 12 September 2019.

https://www.intel.com/content/www/us/en/healthcare-it/article/improved-diagnosis.html. Retrieved 07 September 2019.

http://fortune.com/food-contamination/. Retrieved 22 September 2019.

https://www.intel.com/content/www/us/en/big-data/article/agriculture-harvests-big-data.html. Retrieved 14 September 2019.

CHAPTER 7

Kuroki, H. (2016). How did Archimedes discover the law of buoyancy by experiment?. *Frontiers of Mechanical Engineering, 11*(1), 26–32.

Stein, S. (1999). *Archimedes: what did he do beside cry eureka?* (Vol. 11). MAA.

Dijksterhuis, E. J. (2014). *Archimedes*. Princeton University Press.

Price, H. (1997). *Time's arrow & Archimedes' point: new directions for the physics of time*. Oxford University Press, USA.

Thompson, F. (2008). Archimedes and the golden crown. *Physics Education, 43*(4), 396.

CHAPTER 8

Hunsaker, B. T., & Thomas, D. E. (2017). The Viability Triad: Desirability, Feasibility, and Sustainability as the New Strategic Decision Imperative. *Journal of Management, 5*(2).

CHAPTER 9

https://fas.org/sgp/crs/row/R40213.pdf. Retrieved February 17, 2020.

CHAPTER 10

https://www.youtube.com/watch?v=QK_G97It_JA. Retrieved December 16, 2019.

Della Porta, D., & Diani, M. (2020). *Social movements: An introduction.* John Wiley & Sons.

Gould, R. V. (1991). Multiple networks and mobilization in the Paris Commune, 1871. *American Sociological Review*, 716–729.

Snow, D. A., Zurcher Jr, L. A., & Ekland-Olson, S. (1980). Social networks and social movements: A microstructural approach to differential recruitment. *American sociological review*, 787–801.

Mandela, N. (1990). *Nelson Mandela: The Struggle is My Life: His Speeches and Writings Brought Together with Historical Documents and Accounts of Mandela in Prison by Fellow-prisoners.* Popular Prakashan.

Einwohner, Rachel L. 2007. "Leadership, Authority, and Collective Action: Jewish Resistance in the Ghettos of Warsaw and Vilna." *American Behavioral Scientist* 50(10): 1306–26.

Gamson, William A. 1990. *The Strategy of Social Protest* (2nd ed). Belmont, CA: Wadsworth Publishing.

Einwohner, Rachel L. 2007. "Leadership, Authority, and Collective Action: Jewish Resistance in the Ghettos of Warsaw and Vilna." *American Behavioral Scientist* 50(10): 1306–26.

Robards, B. (2012). Leaving MySpace, joining Facebook:'Growing up'on social network sites. *Continuum, 26*(3), 385–398.

Mustaffa, N., Ibrahim, F., Mahmud, W. A. W., Ahmad, F., Kee, C. P., & Mahbob, M. H. (2011). Diffusion of innovations: The adoption of Facebook among youth in Malaysia. *The Public Sector Innovation Journal, 16*(3), 1–15.

CHAPTER 11

Rogers, E. M. (2010). *Diffusion of innovations.* Simon and Schuster.

Rogers, E. M., & Shoemaker, F. F. (1971). Communication of Innovations; A Cross-Cultural Approach.

Kee, K. F. (2017). Adoption and diffusion. *The international encyclopedia of organizational communication*, 1–14.

Berliner, R. M., Hardman, S., & Tal, G. (2019). Uncovering early adopter's perceptions and purchase intentions of automated vehicles: Insights from early adopters of electric vehicles in California. *Transportation research part F: traffic psychology and behaviour, 60*, 712–722.

Kalantari, M., & Rauschnabel, P. (2018). Exploring the early adopters of augmented reality smart glasses: The case of Microsoft HoloLens. In *Augmented reality and virtual reality* (pp. 229–245). Springer, Cham.

CHAPTER 12
Chung, M. (2019). The message influences me more than others: How and why social media metrics affect first person perception and behavioral intentions. *Computers in Human Behavior, 91*, 271–278.

Desmidt, S., & Heene, A. (2007). Mission statement perception: Are we all on the same wavelength? A case study in a Flemish hospital. *Health Care Management Review, 32*(1), 77–87.

Heath, C., & Heath, D. (2007). *Made to stick: Why some ideas survive and others die.* Random House.

Schwarz, N., Newman, E., & Leach, W. (2016). Making the truth stick & the myths fade: Lessons from cognitive psychology. *Behavioral Science & Policy, 2*(1), 85–95.

Zalocusky, K. A., Ramakrishnan, C., Lerner, T. N., Davidson, T. J., Knutson, B., & Deisseroth, K. (2016). Nucleus accumbens D2R cells signal prior outcomes and control risky decision-making. *Nature, 531*(7596), 642–646.

Damasio, A., & Carvalho, G. B. (2013). The nature of feelings: evolutionary and neurobiological origins. *Nature Reviews Neuroscience, 14*(2), 143–152.

Bechara, A., Damasio, H., & Damasio, A. R. (2000). Emotion, decision making and the orbitofrontal cortex. *Cerebral cortex, 10*(3), 295–307.

https://www.kia.com/us/en/warranty. Retrieved June 13, 2020.

Southerton, D. G. (2012). *Hyundai and Kia motors: The early years and product development.* Don Southerton.

CHAPTER 13
Oyesiku, N. M. (2016). Johan Cruyff (1947–2016). *Neurosurgery, 79*(1), 1–2.

Dyer, J., Gregersen, H., & Christensen, C. M. (2019). *Innovator's DNA, Updated, with a New Preface: Mastering the Five Skills of Disruptive Innovators.* Harvard Business Press.

Wisnioski, M., Hintz, E. S., Kleine, M. S., Fasihuddin, H., Cavagnaro, L. B., McManus, M., ... & Godin, B. (2019). 19 Remaking the Innovator Imperative.

Tuzovic, S., Wirtz, J., & Heracleous, L. (2018). How do innovators stay innovative? A longitudinal case analysis. *Journal of Services Marketing, 32*(1), 34–45.

Rivet, D. J. (2017). Amazon's Superior Innovation: A Study of Amazon's corporate structure, CEO, and reasons behind why it has become the most innovative company in today's market.

McCormick, A., Meijen, C., & Marcora, S. (2015). Psychological determinants of whole-body endurance performance. *Sports medicine, 45*(7), 997–1015.

Andreacci, J. L., Lemura, L. M., Cohen, S. L., Urbansky, E. A., Chelland, S. A., & Duvillard, S. P. V. (2002). The effects of frequency of encouragement on performance during maximal exercise testing. *Journal of sports sciences, 20*(4), 345–352.

Rogers, E., & van Dam, N. (2015). *You the Positive Force in Change: Leveraging Insights from Neuroscience and Positive Psychology*. Lulu Press, Inc.

Daniel, G., & Goleman, D. (2006). Social Intelligence: The New Science of Human Relationships. *Bantam Dell Pub Group*.

van Eerde, W., & Klingsieck, K. B. (2018). Overcoming procrastination? A meta-analysis of intervention studies. *Educational Research Review, 25*, 73–85.

Hunsaker, B. T. (2020). Innovation Bridgers: The new talent imperative. *Thunderbird International Business Review, 62*(4), 385–392.

Eskreis-Winkler, L., & Fishbach, A. (2019). Not learning from failure—The greatest failure of all. *Psychological science, 30*(12), 1733–1744.

Edmondson, A. C. (2011). Strategies for learning from failure. *Harvard business review, 89*(4), 48–55.

Storey, J., & Barnett, E. (2000). Knowledge management initiatives: learning from failure. *Journal of knowledge management*.

https://www.bayer.com/en/research-and-innovation.aspx. Retrieved August 15, 2020.

https://hbr.org/2012/01/finding-great-ideas-in-emergin. Retrieved February 10, 2020.

Sanberg, P. R., Gharib, M., Harker, P. T., Kaler, E. W., Marchase, R. B., Sands, T. D., ... & Sarkar, S. (2014). Changing the academic culture: Valuing patents and commercialization toward tenure and career advancement. *Proceedings of the National Academy of Sciences, 111*(18), 6542–6547.

ABOUT THE AUTHOR

B. Tom Hunsaker, PhD serves as Innovation Dean (including Executive Education, Digital Learning, and the Global Challenge Lab) for the Thunderbird School of Global Management (top-ranked worldwide in its field and a unit of Arizona State University, which ranks #1 in the U.S. for innovation) where he has also been on the global leadership and strategy faculty for nearly a decade. He is a multi-recipient of the school's distinguished teaching award given to its top professor. He previously held leadership positions for global firms in the performance software and analytical sciences industries. Tom's work has been recommended reading in leading universities, applied by thousands of enterprises and their managers and executives, is published in top practitioner outlets such as *Harvard Business Review and MIT Sloan Review*, scholarly journals, and has been featured in popular press globally. His previous books include *Frankly: Effectively Give and Receive Vital Feedback* and *Mindset Positioning: Premier Development Edition*. This is the second of four volumes in the Premier Development series—bringing to life leading-edge methods and proprietary tools, applied the world over, focused on the key growth architecture dimensions: *mindset, innovation, strategy, and execution*. He is also a principal adviser to select game-changer firms, including GloRaise, Inc (a global marketplace to connect entrepreneurs to leading-edge insights and investment capital) and Qualtis Labs. Tom regularly trains or advises Fortune 500 and emerging enterprise leadership and is a noted speaker who has addressed audiences on four continents. He lives with his wife and children in Arizona where they enjoy the outdoors together as much as possible.

Made in the USA
Coppell, TX
02 October 2020